VIPASSANĀ MEDITATION

Lectures on Insight Meditation

Venerable Sayādaw U Janakābhivaṃsa
Chanmyay Yeiktha Meditation Centre
Yangon, Myanmar

VIPASSANĀ MEDITATION
© VENERABLE SAYADĀW U JANAKĀBHIVAṂSA
ISBN 974-89288-2-9
1st. Edition in Thailand   May   1995,   2,000 copies

First Publication in Malaysia   Aug.   1985
BGF Publication in Malaysia   -----   1990
Second Edition Copyright©   -----   1992
Chanmyay Yeiktha Meditation Centre, Myanmar.

The Edition in Malaysia   July   1997, 1,000 copies
For Dhamma Dana

May the sponsor and family experience soon
the wholesome results of their magnificent
act of genersity.
May the merits of their noble support lead
them to the highest happiness.

Reprinted and donated for free distribution by
The Corporate Body of the Buddha Educational Foundation
11F., 55 Hang Chow South Road Sec 1,
Taipei, Taiwan, R.O.C.
1998 July, 35000 Copies

CONTENTS

Preface

Sudassaṃ vajjamaññesaṃ
Attano pana duddasaṃ

Easily seen are others' faults
Hard indeed to see are one's own
Dhpd. 252

The statement is also very relevant for meditators (yogī). A yogī may keep making the same mistakes and yet remain blind to them, until someone sharp and experienced enough comes along and points them out. Again, after sometime, we may forget and need to be reminded.

On the 30th March to 8th April 1983, we were very fortunate to have a very experienced Vipassanā master to hold a retreat at the Malaysian Buddhist Meditation Centre , Penang, to guide, teach, correct and remind us regarding Vipassanā meditation. We all have benefited greatly by his precise instructions, strict discipline and encouraging words.

We have here a compilation of them for the benefit of all Seekers of Uttermost security from bounds. They are the evening lectures delivered by the Sayādaw U Janakābhivamsa for the yogis' benefit. Some are instructions taken mainly from interviews between the Sayādaw and the yogīs. They have been arranged according to their various items to be made into a comprehensive booklet. Some statements are applicable only to those situations concerned and should not be taken too generally.

Special thanks to the Sayādaw for allowing us to print this book and proofreading it himself.

We are also grateful to all who have helped to make this book possible.

Venerable Sujīva
June 1985.

ACKNOWLEDGEMENT

It is my great pleasure that we can publish this new edition of *Vipassanā Meditation* which so far has been printed three times in Malaysia and Myanmar. We are deeply grateful to the Venerable Bhikkhu Sujīva for his tireless efforts to compile and edit my lectures and instructions given for the benefit of yogis in the retreat I conducted in Penang, Malaysia in April 1983.

This new edition was made during my Dhamma-tour in the West in 1992. Bhikkhu Pesala of the Burmese Vihāra, London, rendered me invaluable assistance in this respect. Royce Wiles, my student in meditation, has polished the language in the manuscript that was entered onto computer by U Dhammasubha, a Malaysian bhikkhu, Maung Aung Gyi and Maung Zaw Myint Oo. I thank them all a great deal.

November 5, 1992.

Ashin Janakābhivaṃsa,
Chanmyay Sayadaw.

5

NAMO TASSA BHAGAVATO ARAHATO SAMMĀSAMBUDDHASSA

CHAPTER ONE

HAPPINESS THROUGH RIGHT UNDERSTANDING

Everybody in the world wants happiness and peace. This is the reason why people are seeking the true path which leads them to the cessation of suffering. All kinds of religions in the world arise because of this search. One great religion in the world is Buddhism, it leads people to the cessation of suffering.

The Cause of Suffering

The Lord Buddha found out the cause of suffering (*dukkha*). According to his teachings, everything arises dependent on conditions. Everything in the world has its cause; nothing arises without a cause. When the Buddha wanted to get rid of suffering (*dukkha*), he had to find out the cause. When the cause has been eradicated, there will not be any effect. When the Omniscient Buddha became

enlightened, he discovered that the cause
of suffering is attachment (*tanhā*). The
word '*tanhā*' means greed, lust, desire,
craving and the like. Buddhist scholars
have translated '*tanhā*' into attachment so
that it covers all forms of desire. So in
English, we use the word 'attachment' for
'*tanha*'.

Tanhā or attachment is the cause of
suffering. When there is *tanhā* there is
dukkha (suffering). When a man can
eliminate *tanhā*, he is sure to get rid of
dukkha. This *tanhā* also arises dependent
on a cause. Without a cause, *tanhā* will
not arise. *Tanhā* is a mental state and a
process of mentality which is conditioned.
The Omniscient Buddha discovered that
the cause of attachment (*tanhā*) is wrong
view, i.e. the false view of a soul, a self,
an 'I' or a 'you', a personality or an
individuality known as *sakkāya-diṭṭhi* or
atta- diṭṭhi. So this *sakkāya- diṭṭhi* or *atta-
diṭṭhi* is the cause of *tanhā* which causes
dukkha. Then what is the cause of this
false view (*sakkāya-diṭṭhi* or *atta-diṭṭhi*)?

The Omniscient Buddha pointed out
that ignorance (*moha* or *avijjā* in Pali) of

the natural processes of mentality and physicality is the cause of the false view of a soul or a self. Thus by realisation or right understanding of this dual process in its true nature, we can exterminate ignorance. Then we come to know the Law of Cause and Effect. We can summarise the chain of cause and effect like this: Ignorance is the cause, false view (*sakkāya-diṭṭhi* or *atta-diṭṭhi*) is the effect. False view is the cause, attachment is the effect. Attachment is the cause, suffering is the effect.

Then what we come to know is: if mental and physical processes are rightly understood, that right understanding will do away with ignorance. When ignorance has been eradicated, then there will not be any false view of a soul, a self, a person or a being. When this false view has been destroyed, there will not arise any attachment at all. When attachment has been destroyed, there will not arise any suffering. Then we reach a stage in which all kinds of suffering cease to exist - the cessation of suffering (*Nirodha-sacca*) is attained.

The Cause of False View

We should consider how ignorance of the mind-body processes causes false view of a soul or a self, a person or a being, an 'I' or a 'you'; and how this false view causes attchment to arise. It is because we do not rightly understand this dual process in its true nature that we consider it as a person or a being, a soul or a self. Then, that person, that being, that 'I' or that 'you' has a desire to be rich, or to be a king, a queen, a president, a prime minister or a millionaire. This desire to be a queen or a president etc., is attachment. It arises through the false idea of a person or a being, a soul or a self, an 'I' or a 'you'.

If we want to exterminate this desire or attachment, then we must destroy its cause. What is the cause? The cause of desire or attachment is, as I have explained earlier, the false view or false concept of a person or a being, a soul or a self. So, when the false view has been destroyed, there will not arise any attachment to become a rich man, a king, a president and so on. The desire to be, to get, to have something arises through false view or the false concept of a person or being, an 'I' or a 'you'. When that desire or attachment arises in us, it brings about all kinds of suffering.

When we are attached to our house, a non-living thing, we are worried about our house. If our house is on fire, we feel sad. Sadness is one of the main kinds of suffering. That suffering is caused by our attachment to our house. Then again, when we are attached to our relatives, to our friends, to our children, or to our parents; this attachment also causes us to suffer. When we are attached to our children, we worry about our children's health, education and so on. If our children fail their examinations, we are worried, we feel sorry and sad. This suffering is mental suffering or mental *dukkha,* and is caused by attachment to our children. So, attachment (*tanhā*) is the cause of suffering. Where does this attachment come from? This attachment comes from the false conception of bodily and mental processes as a person or a being, a soul or a self, an 'I' or a 'you'.

When this concept of personality and individuality has been destroyed, there will not be any attachment. When there is no attachment, there will not be any suffering.

See it as it is

The Omniscient Buddha pointed out that by being mindful of this dual process as it really is, we are able to rightly understand its intrinsic nature. When we want to understand something as it really is, we should observe it, watch it, be mindful of it as it really occurs without analysing it, without logical reasoning, without philosophical thinking and without pre-conceptions . We should be very attentive and mindful of it as it really is.

For example - look at a watch. When we do not observe a watch very attentively and carefully we cannot understand it as it is. When we observe it very attentively and closely, then we see its brand, its design and the figures on it. We come to understand that this is a watch; its brand name is Seiko; it has an international time chart etc. However, if we do not observe it as it is, or if our observation is combined with such preconceived ideas as, "I have seen such a watch before and its brand name is Omega", then, as soon as we see this watch, we will take it to be an Omega. Why? Because we do not observe it attentively and closely. We have used the preconceived idea when we saw it, so the preconceived idea leads us to the wrong conclusion regarding the watch. If we put the preconceived idea aside and just observe it attentively and closely, we will understand it as it is - this is a Seiko, it is made in Japan, it also has an international time chart. We will understand it as it is because we had put aside our preconceived idea of "Omega" when we observed it.

In the same way, when we want to rightly understand the mind-body processes in their true nature or as they really are, we must not analyse them or think about them. We must not reason or use any intellectual knowledge, or any preconceived idea. We must leave them aside and pay bare attention to what is happening to the mind-body phenomena as they really are. Then, we can see our mind-body processes as they really are. When our body feels hot, we should note that feeling of heat as heat. When the body feels cold, we should note it as cold. When we feel pain, we should note it as pain. When we feel happy, we should note that happiness. When we feel angry, we should note that anger as anger. When we feel sorrow, we should be mindful of it as sorrow. When we feel sad or disappointed, we should be aware of our emotional state of sadness or disappointment as it is.

Each and every mental and physical process must be observed as it really occurs so that we can rightly understand it in its true nature. That right understanding will lead us to remove ignorance. When ignorance has been removed, then we do not take the mind-body processes to be a person, a being, a soul or a self. If we take these mind-body processes to be just natural processes, then there will not arise any attachment. When the attachment has been destroyed, we are free from all kinds of suffering and have attained the cessation of suffering. So, mindfulness of mind-body processes in their true nature is the way leading to the cessation of suffering. That is way the Omniscient Buddha delivered a discourse on 'The Four Foundations of Mindfulness'.

In this discourse, the Omniscient Buddha teaches us to be mindful of mental and physical phenomena as they really are. There are many ways by which we have to be mindful of the mind-body processes but they can be summarised as follows:

1. Mindfulness of bodily process (*Kāyānupassanā Satipaṭṭhāna*).

2. Mindfulness of feeling or sensation (*Vedanānupassanā Satipaṭṭhāna*).

3. Mindfulness of consciousness (*Cittānupassanā Satipaṭṭhāna*).

4. Mindfulness of mind-objects (*Dhammānupassanā Satipaṭṭhāna*).

Choiceless Awareness

When we are mindful of our mind-body processes, we do not need to choose any mental or physical process as the object of our meditation. The mind will choose the object by it self. If we choose any mental or physical process as the object of meditation, it means we are attached to it. During meditation, the 'noting mind' or the 'observing mind' will choose the object by itself; perhaps a feeling of happiness for our success, or a painful sensation, or the abdominal movement. Though we try to focus the mind on the abdominal movement, the mind does not stay with it if the pain is more distinct or more prominent. The 'noting mind' will go to the pain and observe it because the more distinct feeling takes the mind toward it very strongly. So we need not choose the object but should observe the object that the mind chooses. When pain disappears through attentive and close awareness, the mind will then choose another object which is more distinct. If an itchy sensation on the back is more distinct or more pronounced than the abdominal movement, the mind will go to the feeling of itchiness and observe it as 'itching,

itching, itching'. When the itchy sensation has disappeared by means of strong mindfulness and deep concentration, the mind will choose (for example) the abdominal movement as its object because it is more distinct then the other objects. If happiness is more distinct then the abdominal movement, the mind will choose happiness as its object and observe it as 'happy, happy, happy'. So the principle of *Vipassanā* meditation or mindfulness meditation is to observe, to watch, or to be mindful of all mental or physical phenomena as they really are. This mindfulness meditation is not only very simple and easy, but also very effective in achieving our goal - the cessation of suffering.

When we are taking food, we should be aware of every action, every activity involved in the act of eating. When we stretch out our arm, we must be aware of the movement of stretching. When the hand touches the spoon or the rice, the touching sensation must be observed. When we hold the spoon, the sensation of holding must be observed. When we dip the spoon into the curry, that dipping movement must be observed. When we scoop curry with the spoon, that movement must be observed. In this way, each and every action involved in the act of eating must be observed as it is because every physical process must be thoroughly realised so as to remove ignorance which is the cause of false view. In the same way, while we are taking a bath; while we are working in the office or at home, we must be aware of all the actions or movements involved. When practising walking meditation in a retreat, the movements of the foot such as the lifting movement, the pushing movement and the dropping movement must be closely and precisely observed as they really are.

Labelling

We may need labelling or naming when we are mindful of any object. When we lift our foot to walk, we should label it as 'lifting'. When we push it forward, we should label it as 'pushing'. When we drop it, we should label it as 'dropping'. In this way 'lifting, pushing, dropping;

lifting, pushing, dropping'. Labelling or naming can lead the mind to the object of meditation closely and precisely. It is also very helpful for a meditator to focus his mind on the object of meditation. However, there may be some meditators who need not label or name the object of meditation. Instead, they just observe it. They should just observe the movement of the foot - from the very beginning of the lifting movement up to the end of the dropping movement. The mind must follow the movement of the foot very closely as it is, without thinking or analysing. In this way, one can develop concentration more deeply than ever.

At the beginning of the practice, the mind wanders very often. Whenever the mind wanders, you should follow the mind and observe it. If you are thinking about your family affairs, that thought must be observed as it is, making a mental note, 'thinking, thinking, thinking'. After the initial thought has disappeared, you should resume your walking and noting as usual - 'lifting, pushing, dropping'.

Samatha and Vipassana

Here, we should know the difference between *Samatha* meditation and *Vipassanā* meditation. *Samatha* means concentration, calmness, tranquility. When the mind is deeply concentrated on the object of meditation, the mind becomes calm and tranquil. The purpose of *Samatha* meditation is to attain deep concentration of the mind on a single object. So, the result of *Samatha* meditation is the attainment of deep concentration such as absorption (*appanā-samādhi, jhāna*) or access concentration (*upacāra-samādhi*). When the mind is deeply concentrated on the object of meditation, all the defilements such as lust, greed, hatred, desire, conceit, ignorance and so on are kept away from the mind which is absorbed in the object. When the mind is free from all defilements or hindrances, we feel calm, tranquil, happy and peaceful. The result of *Samatha* meditation, therefore, is some degree of happiness through the attainment of deep concentration such as absorption (*appanā-samādhi, jhāna*) or access concentration *(upacāra-samādhi)* but it does not enable us to rightly understand the mental and physical phenomena as they really are.

A *Samatha* meditator has to make some device or *kasina* as the object of meditation. For instance, to make a colour *kasina*, he has to make a red circle on the wall about two feet from the floor in accordance with the *Visuddhimagga* commentary. He must make the red circle about the size of a plate and the colour must be of pure red, even and smooth. When the device has been made, then he has to sit on the floor about two feet from the wall, look at the red circle and concentrate on it. Should the mind wander, he must not follow the mind but he must bring it to the object of meditation, i.e. the red circle. He must focus the mind on the red circle and observe it as 'red red, red'. This is the way of *Samatha* meditation in brief.

As for *Vipassanā* meditation, the purpose is to attain the cessation of suffering through rightly understanding mental and physical processes in their true nature. For this, we need some degree of concentration. This concentration can be attained through constant and uninterrupted mindfulness of the mind-body process. Thus, we have a variety of objects of meditation: happiness is an object of meditation and so is anger, sorrow, painful sensation, stiffness, numbness and so on. Any mental or physical process can be the object of meditation.

The purpose and the results of *Samatha* and *Vipassanā* meditation are different, as are the methods.

We should go back to what I explained earlier. When we walk, we observe the movement of the foot - the lifting, pushing and dropping. At the beginning of the practice, our mind is not well concentrated on the foot. When the mind wanders, we have to follow it and observe it as it is until that wandering mind has disappeared. Only after it has disappeared, do we note the movement of the foot as usual. When the mind becomes well concentrated on the movement of the foot, what we note is the movement of the lifting, pushing and dropping and we must not be aware of the form of the foot or the form of the body during walking. When the foot is lifted, the mind notes it as lifting, when the foot is pushed forward, the mind notes is as pushing, when the foot is dropped, the mind notes it as dropping. When we come to realise them as natural processes of movement, we also come to realise the mind that notes them. The lifting movement is one process and the mind that notes it is another process. The pushing movement is one process and the mind that notes it is another process. In this way, we thoroughly realise the two processes of mental phenomena and physical phenomena. We rightly understand this dual process as just natural processes of mental and physical phenomena. We do not take them to be a person, a being, an 'I' or a 'you'. Then there will not arise any false concept of personality, individuality, soul, or self. When this false concept has been destroyed, there will not arise any attachment or desire which is the cause of suffering (*dukkha*). So, because attachment does not arise, there will not arise any *dukkha* which is actually the result of the attachment. We attain the cessation of suffering at the moment of experiencing the process of the movement the lifting, pushing and dropping movement - as just a natural process.

As we proceed, our mindfulness becomes more constant, uninterrupted and powerful. As the mindfulness becomes constant and powerful, the concentration becomes deeper and stronger. When the concentration becomes deep and strong, then our realisation or penetrating insight into mental processes and physical processes becomes clear. So we come to realise many series of lifting movements arising and passing away one after another, many series of pushing movements arising and passing away one after another and many series of dropping movements arising and passing away one after another. During such experience, we come to understand that no part of the process is permanent or everlasting. Every process of movement is subject to impermanence (*anicca*) - arising and passing away very swiftly, so it is not a good process; it is bad. Then we come to realise one of the three characteristics of the mental and physical process, i.e. *dukkha*. When we realise the impermanent and suffering nature of this physical process of movement, then we do not take it to be an everlasting entity - a person, a being, a soul or a self. This is the realisation of the *anatta*, no-soul, no-self, non-ego nature of bodily and mental processes. So we realise the three characteristics of mental and physical phenomena, impermanence (*anicca*), suffering (*dukkha*) and no-soul or no-self (*anatta*).

Realisation of the Noble Truths

In this manner, a meditator goes through all the stages of insight knowledge of mental and physical processes one after another. After the last stage has been reached, he has attained enlightenment of the First Path, *Sotāpatti-magga*. At the moment of attaining the First Path the meditator realises the Four Noble Truths:-

Dukkha-sacca   The Truth of Suffering
Samudaya-sacca The Truth of the Cause
of suffering

Nirodha-sacca	The Truth of the Cessation of Suffering
Magga-sacca	The Truth of the Way Leading to the Cessation of Suffering

When he realises the ever changing phenomena of mentality and physicality, it means that he has realised the Truth of Suffering. As a result, attachment, which is the cause of suffering, is removed and the meditator has reached the state in which suffering ceases to exist.

The Noble Eightfold Path

At that moment he has completely developed the Noble Eightfold Path:-

1.	*Sammā-diṭṭhi*	Right Understanding
2.	*Sammā-saṅkappa*	Right Thought
3.	*Sammā-vācā*	Right Speech
4.	*Sammā-kammanta*	Right Action
5.	*Sammā-ājīva*	Right Livelihood
6.	*Sammā-vāyāma*	Right Effort
7.	*Sammā-sati*	Right Mindfulness
8.	*Sammā-samādhi*	Right Concentration

From the time he can concentrate the mind to a large extent on the object of meditation, i.e. mental-physical processes, he is developing this Noble Eightfold Path (though not completely). How? When he focuses the mind on the movement of the foot, he has to make a mental effort; that mental effort is 'Right Effort' (*Sammā-vāyāma*). Because of that mental effort, he can focus his mind so that he can be mindful of the movement of the foot. That mindfulness is 'Right Mindfulness' (*Sammā-sati*) because it leads him to the right understanding of the mental and physical processes. When his mind is focused on the movement of the foot, it is concentrated on it for a moment but when the concentration become continuous and constant, stronger and deeper, that concentration is 'Right Concentration' (*Sammā-samādhi*). It is natural for the mind to wander in the beginning of the practice. However much effort a meditator makes, the mind does not stay with the movement of the foot at first. Then, one of the mental states which arises together with the mindfulness of the movement of

the foot leads the mind to the object of
meditation, i.e. the movement of the foot.
That mental state which leads the mind
to the object of meditation is 'Right
Thought' (*Sammā-sankappa*). The
characteristic of 'Right Thought' is the
directing of the mind to the object of
meditation. In this way, the mind
becomes well concentrated on the object
of meditation, the movement of the foot.
Then, it penetrates into the true nature
of the physical process of the movement
- knowing it as a natural process. That
knowing or that understanding of it as a
natural process is 'Right Understanding'
(*Sammā-diṭṭhi*). Thus we have developed
five mental factors of the Noble Eightfold
Path when we are mindful of the
movement of the foot. These are:-

1. *Sammā-vāyāma*   Right Effort
2. *Sammā-sati*   Right Mindfulness
3. *Sammā-samādhi*   Right Concentration
4. *Sammā-sankappa*   Right Thought
5. *Sammā-diṭṭhi*   Right Understanding

These five mental factors are included in mindfulness of the mind-body processes as they are. While engaged in mindfulness meditation, we abstain from wrong speech, wrong action and wrong livelihood. Abstention from wrong speech means 'Right Speech' (*Sammā-vācā*) abstention from wrong actions means 'Right Action' (*Sammā -kammanta*); abstention from wrong livelihood means 'Right Livelihood' (*Sammā - ājīva*). So we have altogether the eight mental factors of the Noble Eightfold Path while we are being mindful of any mental or physical process. As we develop the Noble Eightfold Path, we can remove false view (*sakkāya- diṭṭhi* or *atta-diṭṭhi*) by the power of Right Understanding (*Sammā-diṭṭhi*), one of the factors of the Noble Eightfold Path. So when a meditator enters into the First Path, *Sotāpatti-magga*, he has completely developed the Noble Eightfold Path - *Magga-sacca*, the way leading to the cessation of suffering. This is how he has realised the Four Noble Truths by means of cultivating mindfulness of mental and physical processes in their true nature.

CHAPTER TWO

PRELIMINARY INSTRUCTIONS FOR MEDITATORS

In the teachings of the Buddha, there are three kinds of training:-

Training in moral conduct (*sīla*),
Training in concentration (*samādhi*), and
Training in wisdom, insight or enlightenment (*paññā*).

When we practise moral conduct, it means having restraint in speech and actions, i.e. observing at least the five precepts or eight precepts as laymen, and for the *Sangha* (community of monks), the 227 precepts or rules of training known as the *Pātimokkha*. When we abstain from unwholesome actions and speech, we observe these precepts completely.

When we observe the five precepts, we have to abstain from killing, stealing, sexual misconduct, telling lies and using any kind of intoxicant.

The first precept, abstention from killing, means refraining from unwholesome actions. The second precept, abstention from stealing and illegal possession of things not given by the owner, means refraining from unwhole-some actions. It is the same with the third and fifth precepts, i.e. abstention from sexual misconduct and intoxicants. The fourth precept, abstention from telling lies is refraining from false and unwholesome speech. Therefore, if we refrain from unwholesome speech and actions, our *sīla* is fully observed.

During a meditation retreat, you have to observe the eight precepts so that you can have more time to devote to meditation.

The sixth precept means abstention from taking food after noon (until dawn the next morning). Although you must refrain from taking any kind of food during these hours, you can take honey and certain kinds of fruit juice such as orange and lemon juices.

To observe the seventh precept, you must refrain from dancing, singing, playing and listening to music and adorning yourself with anything which will beautify yourself such as using flowers, perfumes and so on.

The eighth precept is abstention from high and luxurious beds. The third of the eight precepts refers to abstention from any kind of sexual contact, and not just from sexual misconduct. By refraining from these activities, your speech and actions are pure. These are the eight precepts you will have to observe during your retreat.

Observing eight precepts means purification of moral conduct - *Sīla-visuddhi*. *Sīla-visuddhi* is a prerequisite for a meditator to make progress in meditative practice. When moral conduct is purified, one never feels guilty. When one does not feel guilty, one's mind becomes steady, thereby, one can easily attain deep concentration of mind (*samādhi*) which, in turn, gives rise to insight wisdom (*paññā*).

What is Vipassana?

Vipassana is a *Dhamma* term which is a combination of two words. 'Vi' is one word, '*passanā*' is the other. Here, '*vi*' refers to the three characteristics of mentality and physicality, i.e. impermanence . (*anicca*), unsatisfactoriness or suffering (*dukkha)* and no-soul, no-self or non-ego (*anatta*).

'*Passanā*' means right understanding or realisation through deep concentration, or right understanding of the three characteristics of mentality (*nāma*) and physicality (*rūpa*). When we practise *Vipassanā* meditation or mindfulness meditation, the purpose is to realise, *anicca, dukkha* and *anatta* - the three characteristics of phenomena.

By realising these three characteristics of mentality and physicality, we can exterminate every defilement such as lust, greed, desire, craving, hatred, ill-will, jealousy, conceit, sloth and torpor, sorrow and worry, restlessness and remorse. Having destroyed all these defilements, we then attain deliverance or the cessation of suffering. As long as we have any of these defilements, we are sure to experience many kinds of *dukkha* (suffering). Defilements (*kilesas*) are the cause of suffering, therefore, when defilements have been destroyed, all kinds of suffering cease to exist.

Mindfulness of the Four Elements

During the practice, we must observe each and every mental and physical process which is arising at the moment. In the beginning of the practice, we must contemplate the abdominal movements as instructed by the Most Venerable Mahāsī Sayādaw. Contemplation of the abdominal movements is in accordance with the *Mahā Satipaṭṭhāna Sutta*, the Discourse on the Four Foundations of Mindfulness. In that discourse, there is a chapter concerning mindfulness of the four elements. There the Buddha teaches us to be mindful of the four elements when they arise (*paṭhavī-dhātu* - earth element, *āpo-dhātu* - water element, *tejo-dhātu* - fire element and *vāyo-dhātu* - wind element). Not only these four elements but all mental and physical phenomena must be observed.

We must understand that the earth element is not actually the earth. Instead it refers to the true nature of the earth element. Earth element is the name given to its individual characteristics, such as hardness and softness. The scriptures say, "Hardness and softness are the individual or specific characteristics of the earth element" - so when you thoroughly realise hardness or softness in any part of your body, it means that you are realising the true nature or individual characteristic of the earth element (*paṭhavī-dhātu*).

Water element is not actually water but the term given to the individual characteristics of the element. Fluidity and cohesion are characteristics of the water element (*āpo-dhātu*). When you realise the nature of fluidity or cohesion in any part of your body, it means you are realising the water element. Similarly, the fire element is not really fire, but the specific characteristic of the element. Heat and cold are the specific characteristics of the fire element (*tejo-dhātu*). Wind element (*vāyo-dhātu*) likewise is not wind but the term given to the specific characteristics of the wind element, that is, movement, motion, vibration or support in any part of your body. When you feel, realise and rightly understand this movement, motion, vibration or supporting nature in any part of your body, it means that you are realising the wind element. This is mindfulness of the four elements.

The Omniscient Buddha said, "Any mental or physical process must be observed as it is." When we sit in any comfortable position and focus our mind on the mental and physical processes, we may not know which object must be observed first. So, to overcome this difficulty, the Most Venerable Mahāsī Sayādaw instructed his meditators to begin with the abdominal movements. When we breathe in, the abdomen rises, when we breathe out, the abdomen falls. We should focus our mind on the abdominal movement. When the abdomen rises, we should note it as 'rising', and when it falls, as 'falling'. In this way: 'rising, falling, rising, falling'. Thus we can feel the inward and outward movement of the abdomen. This specific characteristic of *vāyodhātu* must be thoroughly realised by meditators so that they can destroy the false view of a person, a being or a soul. They must observe the inward movement and outward movement of the abdomen or the rising and falling movement of the abdomen, making a mental note of 'rising, falling, rising, falling'.

During the contemplation of your abdominal movement, when you hear a sound which is loud enough to be noted, then you should note, 'hearing, hearing, hearing'. At the beginning of the practice, you may not overcome it, so you should note, 'hearing, hearing' as much as possible. When you think it is enough for you to stop, then you should return to the primary object, the abdominal movement. Sometimes the sound may last for a second or two. Then, when the sound has disappeared, your mind will naturally go back to the primary object, 'rising' and 'falling' which you should note as usual.

Mindfulness of Mental and Emotional States

When you feel happy or unhappy, or when you feel sorry and sad, these emotional states must be observed as they really are - mentally noting, 'happy, happy' or 'unhappy, unhappy' or 'sad, sad', and so on. After the emotional state has disappeared, the noting mind naturally returns to the abdominal movement, which should be observed as usual. When your mind goes out and thinks about your work, your family or your relatives, you must leave the abdominal movement alone and observe the wandering thoughts, making a mental note 'thinking, thinking'. You should be careful at this point. When you observe any mental state or emotional state, your noting mind must be energetic, attentive, precise and somewhat quick so that it becomes continuous, uninterrupted and constant. When the noting mind becomes powerful, the thought or idea, or the thinking mind 'stops' by itself. Then the noting mind no longer has the object to note. It naturally returns to the abdominal movement which should be noted as usual.

Walking Meditation

The Buddha said that mindfulness must be applied to the four postures of the body, i.e. walking, standing, sitting and lying down.

While you are walking, you must be mindful of it as it is-

While you are standing, you must be mindful of it as it is-

While you are sitting, you must be mindful of it as it is-

While you are lying down, you must be mindful of it as it is.

So, in every posture, there must be mindfulness.

We instruct meditators to practise walking and sitting meditation alternately so that they can concentrate more easily and hence attain insight into the walking and sitting processes. Every session of sitting must be preceded by walking because in walking meditation, the movement of the foot is more distinct than the abdominal movement is when sitting. When your meditation practce matures, you may then need sitting meditation for a longer period than walking. When you have reached the sixth stage of insight knowledge, you may practise sitting meditation longer than walking; you may sit for two or three hours and walk one hour. At that stage, your concentration is good, deep and strong enough to realise the dissolution of *nāma* and *rūpa* (mental and physical phenomena). But in the beginning of the practice, you need walking meditation longer than sitting because you are not yet able to sit for long but can walk longer. You can attain some degree of concentration more easily in walking than in sitting.

So first of all, you should practise walking meditation by being aware of stepping. When you make a left step, note it as 'left'. When you make a right step, note it as 'right'. In this way, note 'left, right, left, right', or just 'stepping, stepping'. Labelling or naming is not so important as the mind that observes the movement of the foot. You should lay stress on awareness, sharp awareness of the movement of the foot.

When you practise walking meditation, you must not close your eyes. Instead, your eyes must be half-closed (that means, relax and keep your eyes normal) and you should look at a place on the floor about four or five feet in front of your foot.

You must not bend your head too low. If you bend your head too low, you will soon feel tension in your neck or shoulders. Also, you may have a headache or dizziness. You must not look at your foot. If you look at your foot, you cannot concentrate well on the movement. Nor must you look around here and there. Once you look around, the mind goes with the eyes; then your concentration breaks. You may have a tendency or desire to look around when you feel that someone is coming towards you or passing in front of you. That tendency or desire to look around must be very attentively observed and noted as 'tendency' or 'wanting to look' until it has disappeared. When the tendency or desire has disappeared, you won't look around. Then you can maintain your concentration. So, please be careful not to look around so that you can maintain your concentration and make progress in your attainment of concentration by walking meditation. Your hands should be locked together in front or behind. If you feel you should change the position of your hands, you may do so, but mindfully.

When you have an intention to change position, you should note 'intending, intending'. Even then, you should change the position very slowly and every action and movement involved in the act of changing must be observed. You must not be unmindful of any movement or action. When you have changed the position of your hands, then you should continue to note the movements of the foot as before.

In sitting meditation too, those who have some experience in meditational

practice should sit at least 45 minutes
without changing position. Beginners should
sit at least 20-30 minutes without changing
position. If a beginner is unable to bear the
severe pain which arises, he may feel like
changing his posture. Before doing so, he
must note the intention to change posture,
as 'intending, intending'. Then he should
change his posture very, very slowly being
aware of all the movements and actions
involved in the changing of postures. When
he has changed his posture, he should then
return to the abdominal movement, the
primary object, and note as usual.

Silent Awareness

In a meditation retreat, you must not
do any action or movement quickly. You
must slow down all actions and movements
as much as possible so that you can apply
mindfulness to every minute movement or
action of the body. At home, you need not
slow down all these actions and movements
but rather, they should be normal, and
mindfully observed. All actions and
movements must be mindfully noted as they
really are. That is general mindfulness. In a
retreat, you must slow down all actions and

movements because you have nothing else to do except to be mindful of all your mental and physical activities. You must not talk, except for the few words which are necessary in your daily routine, but these few words should also be spoken slowly and softly so that your words do not disturb the concentration of other meditators. You should do everything with very little noise or without any noise. You must not make a sound by walking sluggishly and heavily. If you are mindful of the movements of your foot, you won't make any sound when walking.

You must be mindful of whatever arises in your body and mind. You must be aware of any activity of your mind and body as it really is. As you are eating, you must be mindful of all the actions and movements in eating. When you are taking a bath, dressing or drinking water, you must slow down all your actions and observe the movements. When you sit down, you should do it very slowly, being aware of the whole movement of sitting. When you stand up, that must also be done very slowly by being aware of the movement because we want to realise every mental or physical process in its true nature. All mental and physical processes are ever changing - appearing and disappearing, arising and vanishing. We want to realise this true nature of mental and physical processes. Therefore, we should slow down all actions and movements.

Mindfulness and concentration will pave the way for insight to unfold. When mindfulness becomes continuous, naturally the concentration becomes deeper. When the concentration becomes deeper, insight will unfold by itself. Therefore, we should strive to have constant and continuous mindfulness.

CHAPTER THREE

SEVEN BENEFITS OF MINDFULNESS MEDITATION

Seven benefits of Mindfulness meditation as taught by the Buddha are recorded in the *Mahā Satipaṭṭhāna Sutta* - the Discourse on the Four Foundations of Mindfulness. But before I deal with them, I want to explain to you briefly the four aspects of Buddhism. These four aspects are:-

1. Devotional aspect of Buddhism,

2. Ethical aspect of Buddhism,

3. Moral aspect of Buddhism,

4. Practical aspect of Buddhism (including the experiential aspect).

Devotional Aspect

The devotional aspect of Buddhism means 'rites and rituals', chanting of *suttas* and *parittas*, offering of flowers and incense as well as offering of food and robes. When we perform such good deeds, we do so with *sraddhā* (in Sanskrit) or *saddhā* (in Pāḷi).

The word *saddhā* is difficult to translate into English. There is no English equivalent for the Pāli word '*saddhā*'. If we translate *saddhā* to be faith, the word 'faith' does not cover the real sense, and if we translate it as 'confidence', it also does not cover the real sense of '*saddhā*'. We cannot find a single word in English which can give a complete meaning of *saddhā*. To me, *saddhā* can be taken to mean belief through right understanding of the *Dhamma*.

When we perform religious ceremonies we do it with a belief in the Triple Gem (*Tiratana*). We believe in the *Buddha*, the *Dhamma* (his teachings) and the *Sangha* (the Order of Buddhist monks). We hold the view that the Buddha has eradicated all defilements through his supreme enlightenment, so he is worthy of respect (an *Arahant*). He was a *Buddha* because he had strived and was enlightened by himself, not because he learned the *Dhamma* from any teacher. We believe in the *Buddha* in this way. The Buddha taught us to live happily and peacefully and he taught us the way leading to the cessation of all kinds of sufferings. We believe that if we follow his teaching or his way, we are sure to live happily and peacefully and to get rid of suffering. For this reason, we believe in the *Dhamma*. In the same way, we believe in the *Sangha*. When we say *Sangha*, it mainly means the *Ariya-sangha*, the Noble *Sangha* who have attained any one of the four stages of the Path (*magga*). But in the general sense, it also refers to the *Sammuti-sangha* (those who are still striving to eradicate the defilements). Thus we pay homage to the Triple Gem (*Tiratana*) - the *Buddha, Dhamma* and *Sangha*. We also believe that by chanting *suttas* and *parittas* as taught by the Buddha, we perform meritorious deeds which will be conducive to the cessation of suffering. Performing these meritorious deeds forms the devotional aspect of Buddhism. However, we should not be content with this devotional aspect if we want to enjoy the essence of Buddhism and be free from all kinds of suffering. Therefore, we must proceed to practise the higher aspects.

Ethical Aspect

The second aspect of Buddhism is the ethical aspect. This is following the

Buddha's teaching regarding our actions, speech and mental purification. There are many doctrines concerned with the ethical aspect of Buddhism.

By following these doctrines, we can lead a happy life in this existence as well as the next but we cannot yet be rid of suffering totally. The ethical aspects of Buddhism are:-

1. Refraining from all kinds of evil deeds,

2. Performing meritorious or good deeds,

3. Purifying the mind from all kinds of defilements.

These are the three parts of the ethical aspect of what the Omniscient Buddha has taught us and they are the exhortations of all the Buddhas. If we follow these doctrines, we can lead a happy and peaceful life because Buddhism is founded on the Law of Cause and Effect. If we refrain from all kinds of evil deeds, we will not suffer any bad results.

As to the purificaation of mind from defilements, we have to practise *Samatha* meditation as well as *Vipassanā* meditation. With *Samatha* meditation our mind can be purified only while it is engaged in the meditative practice, but when it is not, defilements will attack us again. If we purify our minds through the realisation of the mind-body processes in their true nature, the defilements will not return. Realisation or insight into mental and physical phenomena is known as *Vipassanā-ñāṇa* (insight knowledge). It overcomes some aspects of defilements and reduces defilements such as greed, anger, delusion and so on. Certain defilements which have been destroyed by means of *Vipassanā-ñāṇa* (penetrative insight) will not be able to attack us again. In other words, when we have experienced insight knowledge, that experience will not disappear or go away from us. When we reflect on the experience we have had during meditation, the insight that we attained comes to us again, and with this insight, some aspects of defilements abandoned by insight will not arise again. Thus, we can purify our minds from some defilements. But if we have enough *saddhā*, we will put forth greater effort in our practice and attain the Fourth Path, *Arahantship*. Then we can exterminate every defilement. When the defilements have been totally destroyed and the mind completely purified there will not arise any *dukkha* or suffering. Suffering ceases to exist. This purification of the mind from defilements is concerned with the practical aspect of Buddhism whereas the former two points are concerned with the ethical aspect of Buddhism.

There is also the *Mangala Sutta* (*Sutta-nipāta*, verses 258-269) with 38 kinds of blessings. In the *suttas* are many ethics to follow which enable us to live happily and peacefully such as:-

> You should live in a suitable place where you can be prosperous in every aspect, having done meritorious deeds in the past.

> You should do meritorious deeds as much as possible at present too.

> You must watch your deeds, speech and mind properly.

That means, we should keep our deeds, speech and thoughts free from defilements. In this way, we have many aspects of ethics to follow so that we can live happily and peacefully.

I want to remind you of the *Ambalaṭṭhika Rāhulovādasutta (Majjhima-nikāya, Sutta* No. 61) which may be familiar to you. In that *sutta*, the Buddha encouraged his son, Rāhula, who was a seven year old *sāmanera*, to live properly, happily and peacefully. The Buddha taught Rāhula to stop and reflect whenever he had the intention of doing something.

> Rāhula, you must be mindful of what you are going to do and consider whether this deed will be harmful to yourself or to others. By considering thus, if you find that this deed will be harmful to yourself or to others, you must not do it. But if this deed will not be harmful to yourself or to others, you may do it.

In this way, the Buddha instructed Rāhula to consider what is to be done, to be aware of what is being done and to reflect on what has been done. So this ethic too is the best way for living happily and peacefully in our daily life. There are innumerable aspects of ethics conducive to a happy and peaceful life. If we try to understand these ethics and follow them, we are sure to live a happy and peaceful life although we cannot yet get rid of all our suffering.

Moral Aspect

Though these ethics are very conducive to a happy and peaceful life, we should not be contented merely with the second aspect of Buddhism. We should proceed to the higher aspects of Buddhism, the third aspect - the moral aspect. In the moral aspect, you must observe precepts, either five, eight or ten. The ten precepts are for novices (*sāmaneras*) while the 227 rules are for monks (*bhikkhus*). In daily life, we must observe at least the five precepts. When we can observe the five precepts perfectly, our morality is purified. When moral conduct is purified, a meditator can easily practise meditation, either

Samatha or *Vipassanā* meditation. Based on purification of moral conduct, a meditator can easily concentrate on the object of meditation and gain deep concentration, whereby the mind is clear, serene and happy.

Practical Aspect

Next, we have the fourth aspect, i.e. the practical aspect of Buddhism. We must practise meditation so that we can deliver ourselves from defilements and, as a result, attain the cessation of all kinds of suffering. Here, we practise two kinds of meditation which make up the practical aspect of Buddhism - one to enable us to attain deep concentration, and the other to enable us to attain the cessation of suffering through the realisation of mentality and physicality in their true nature. The Buddha stressed the second type of meditation - *Vipassanā* meditation. When we practise *Vipassanā* meditation, we have to follow the *Mahā Satipaṭṭhāna Sutta*, the discourse on the Four Foundations of Mindfulness. If we apply mindfulness to all our mind-body processes, we are sure to attain the cessation of suffering. The Buddha described the four Foundations of Mindfulness when he gave the discourse on *Mahā Satipaṭṭhāna Sutta* in Kuru province.

Seven Benefits of Meditation

In the introductory passage of that *sutta*, the Buddha explained the seven benefits which a meditator can gain through his own experience of *Dhamma*.

The First Benefit is purification. When a person practises mindfulness, he can purify his being from all defilements. The Pali word '*kilesa*' may be familiar to you. The word '*kilesa*' is translated as defilements by Buddhist scholars. The *kilesa* are of ten main kinds:-

Lobha	*Vicikicchā*
Dosa	*Thīna-middha*
Moha	*Uddhacca-kukkucca*
Diṭṭhi	*Ahirika*
Māna	*Anottappa*

·*Lobha* means not only greed but also desire, lust, craving, attachment and love. When one of these mental states arises in us, our mind gets defiled. So these are known as defilements.

> *Dosa* is hatred, anger, ill-will or aversion.
> *Moha* is delusion or ignorance.
> *Diṭṭhi* is wrong view or false view.
> *Māna* is conceit.
> *Vicikicchā* is sceptical doubt.

Thina-middha is sloth and torpor. Sleepiness also comes under sloth and torpor. Sloth and torpor are 'old friends' of meditators and also those who listen to the *Dhamma*.

Today, during interview, all the meditators reported the experience: 'I am tired, I feel sleepy'. At the beginning of the practice, we have to struggle because we have not yet become accustomed to the task of mindfulness meditation. This is a critical stage of meditation, but it will not last long. It may last for two or three days. After three days, all meditators will be alright. They will not find it too difficult to overcome these 'old friends' which are obstructing their progress in concentration as well as insight.

Uddhacca   kukkucca means restlessness and remorse.

Ahirika means moral shamelessness. One who is not ashamed of evil deeds in speech, thought and action.

Anottappa means moral fearlessness -that is one is not afraid of evil deeds in speech, thought and action. This moral fearlessness is one of the defilements.

These are the ten kinds of defilements which must be abandoned or removed from our minds by means of *Vipassanā* meditation. The Buddha says:-

If one practises mindfulness meditation, one can be purified from all defilements.

That means, he can attain *Arahantship* when he is completely purified from all kinds of defilements. This is the first benefit.

The Second Benefit of mindfulness is the overcoming of sorrow and worry.

You will not be worried about failure, or be sorry about the death of your relatives, or about the loss of your work. You will not be sorry about anything if you practise this mindfulness meditation. Although you have not attained any Path and Fruition(*magga* and *phala*), you can overcome sorrow and worry to some extent, because when sorrow or worry arises, you will be mindful of it as it is. When mindfulness becomes powerful, that worry or sorrow will stop and disappear. When you have completely developed mindfulness meditation, you are sure to attain *Arahantship*, and hence be free from worry and sorrow permanently. In this way, worry and sorrow can be overcome by mindfulness meditation.

The Third Benefit is that of overcoming lamentation. Although your parents, children or relatives die, you will not have any lamentation for them because you have fully realised that mental and physical processes constitute the so-called 'child' or the so-called 'parents'. In this way, lamentation can be overcome by mindfulness meditation. Regarding the third benefit, the commentary on the *Mahā Satipaṭṭhāna Sutta* mentions a story:-

A woman, named Patācārā, whose husband, two sons, parents and brothers had died within a day or two, went mad due to sorrow, worry and lamentation. She was overwhelmed by sorrow over the death of the people she loved.

The commentary mentions this story as proof that one can overcome sorrow, worry and lamentation by means of mindfulness meditation.

One day, the Buddha was giving a discourse to an audience at Jetavana monastery near Savatthi. Then this mad woman, who was going for a stroll, went into the monastery and saw the audience listening to the discourse. She approached the audience. An old man, who was very kind to the poor, took off his upper robe, threw it to the woman and said to her, "Dear daughter, please use my robe to cover your body." At the same time the Buddha said to her, "Dear sister, be mindful." Because of the soothing voice of the Buddha, the mad woman come to her senses. She then sat at the edge of the audience and listened to the discourse. The Buddha, knowing that she had come to her senses, aimed his discourse at her. Listening to the discourse given by the Buddha, the woman's mind gradually absorbed the essence of the doctrine. When her mind was well prepared to realise the *Dhamma*, the Buddha expounded the Four Noble Truths:-

Dukkha-sacca	The Truth of Suffering
Samudaya-sacca	The Truth of the Cause of Suffering
Nirodha-sacca	The Truth of the Cessation of Suffering
Magga-sacca	The Truth of the Way Leading to the Cessation of Suffering

The Fourth Noble Truth includes advice on how to be mindful of whatever arises in our mind and body as it really is.

Patācārā, having come to her senses, rightly understood the technique of mindfulness, applied it to whatever arose in the mind-body processes and to whatever she heard. As her mindfulness gained momentum, her concentration became deeper and stronger. Because her concentration became deep, her insight and penetrating knowledge of the mind-body processes became powerful, and she gradually realised both the specific characteristics and common characteristics of mental and physical phenomena. Thus she progressively experienced all the stages of insight knowledge while listening to the discourse, and attained the First Path, *Sotāpatti-magga*. Through her own personal experience fo the *Dhamma* by means of mindfulness meditation, the sorrow, worries and lamentation she had had, totally disappeared from her mind, and she became a 'new woman'. Thus she overcome her worry, sorrow and lamentation by means of mindfulness meditation. So the commentary on the *Mahā Satipaṭṭhāna Sutta* mentioned. Not only the people during the time of the Buddha, but also people nowadays can overcome sorrow and worry if they practise this mindfulness meditation to attain some higher stages of insight. You are also included in those people who can overcome sorrow and worry by means of mindfulness meditation.

The Fourth Benefit is the cessation of physical suffering.

The Fifth Benefit is the cessation of mental suffering.

Physical suffering such as pain, stiffness, itchiness, numbness and so on can be overcome by this mindfulness in meditation retreats as well as in daily life. When you have some experience in the meditation practice, you can overcome your mental and physical suffering to a large extent. If you invest enough effort and time you can exterminate both mental and physical suffering permanently when you have attained *Arahantship*. But during meditaion, you can overcome pain, stiffness, numbness, itchiness and all kinds of unpleasant physical sensations by observing them very attentively and closely. Therefore, you need not be afraid of pain, stiffness or numbness because these are your 'good friends' who can help you to attain the cessation of suffering If you observe the pain energetically, precisely and closely, it may seem more severe because you know it more and more clearly. When you have comprehended the unpleasantness of this painful sensation, you will not identify it with yourself because the sensation is perceived as just a natural process of mental phenomena. You are not attached to the painful sensation as 'I' or 'mine' or 'me', or a 'person' or a 'being'. In this way, you can eradicate the wrong view of a soul, a self, a person, a being, an 'I' or a 'you'.

When the root of all kinds of defilements, i.e. *sakkāya-diṭṭhi* or *atta-diṭṭhi* has been destroyed you are sure to attain the First Path, *Sotāpatti-magga*. Then you can proceed with your practice to attain the three higher stages of the Path and Fruition. That is why I say that unpleasant physical sensations such as pain, stiffness and numbness are your 'good friends' who can help you to attain the cessation of suffering. In other words,

this numbness or any painful sensation
is the key to the door of *nibbāna*. When
you feel pain, you are lucky. Pain is the
most valuable object of meditation because
it attracts the 'noting mind' to stay with
it for a very long time. The 'noting mind'
can concentrate on it deeply and be
absorbed in it. When the mind is
completely absorbed in the painful
sensation, you will no longer be aware of
your bodily form or yourself. It means you
are realising the *sabhāva-lakkhana* of the
pain or the individual characteristic of the
painful sensation (*dukkha-vedanā*).
Proceeding with the practice you will be
able to realise the common characteristics
of impermanence, suffering and no-soul
or no-self nature of mental and physical
phenomena. Then that will lead you to the
cessation of all kinds of sufferings. So you
are lucky if you have pain.

In Burma, some meditators, having
passed the third stage of insight knowledge
(*sammasana-ñāṇa*), almost completely
overcame all painful sensations. but were
dissatisfied with their practice because
they had no pain to note. So they folded

their legs under themselves and pressed them so that they could get pain. They were looking for their 'good friend' who could lead them to the cessation of suffering.

When you feel unhappy, please observe that unhappiness insistently, attentively and very closely as 'unhappy, unhappy'. If you feel depressed, that depression must be observed very attentively and perseveringly. When your mindfulness becomes powerful, the unhappiness and depression will cease to exist. So the overcoming of mental suffering is the fifth benefit of mindfulness meditation.

The Sixth Benefit is the attainment of enlightenment, the Path and Fruition (*magga* and *phala*). When you devote enough time and effort to your mindfulness meditation, you will attain at least the First Path, *Sotāpatti-magga*. This is the sixth benefit of mindfulness meditation.

The Seventh Benefit is that you are sure to attain *nibbāna*, deliverance, emancipation through mindfulness meditation.

The seven kinds of benefits of mindfulness meditation which the *Vipassanā* meditator can gain through personal experience of *Dhamma:-*

1. Purification from all kinds of defilements.
2. Overcoming sorrow and worry.
3. Overcoming lamentation.
4. Cessation of all kinds of physical suffering.
5. Cessation of all kinds of mental suffering.
6. Attainment of enlightenment.
7. Attainment of *nibbāna*.

The Buddha began the *Mahā Satipaṭṭhāna Sutta* with these seven benefits of mindfulness meditation. So you are sure to acquire these seven benefits if you put strenuous effort into your practice.

We are lucky because we believe in the Buddha who is enlightened and who teaches the right way which leads to the cessation of suffering. But we should not be complacent. In the Pāli texts, there is a simile:-

There is a great pond full of clear water with many lotus flowers in it. A traveller's hands are dirty. He knows that if he washes them in the pond, they will be clean. But though he knows it, he does not go to the pond to wash his hands, his hands are still dirty. In this way, he passes the pond and continues his journey.

Then the question was asked in the text: "If the man remains dirty, who is to be blamed, the pond or the traveller?" Obviously, the traveller. Though he knew he could wash the dirt away in the pond, he did not do it. Therefore, the traveller is to be blamed. The Buddha teaches us the way of mindfulness. If we know the way but do not practise this mindfulness meditation, we will not get rid of suffering. If we do not get rid of suffering, who should be blamed? The Buddha, the way of mindfulness, or us? Yes, we should be blamed. If you practise this mindfulness meditation with strenuous effort, you will purify yourself from all defilements and get rid of suffering by obtaining these seven kinds of benefits of mindfulness meditation.

CHAPTER FOUR

THE FOUR FOUNDATIONS OF MINDFULNESS

When the Buddha had explained the seven benefits of mindfulness, he continued to explain the Four Foundations of Mindfulness:-

1. *Kāyānupassanā Satipaṭṭhāna*
2. *Vedanānupassanā Satipaṭṭhāna*
3. *Cittānupassanā Satipaṭṭhāna*
4. *Dhammānupassanā Satipaṭṭhāna*

Kāyānupassanā Satipaṭṭhāna means contemplation of the body or mindfulness of any bodily process as it occurs. *Vedanānupassanā Satipaṭṭhāna* means contemplation of feeling or sensation. This feeling or sensation is of three types:-

(a) Pleasant feeling or sensation,

(b) Unpleasant feeling or sensation,

(c) Neutral feeling or sensation.

Pleasant feeling or pleasant sensation is called *sukha-vedanā* (*sukha* means pleasant, *vedanā* is feeling or sensation). Unpleasant sensation or unpleasant feeling is called *dukkha-vedanā* in Pali (*dukkha* here means unpleasant). Neutral feeling or neutral sensation is called *upekkhā-vedanā* (*upekkhā* means neutral - neither pleasant nor unpleasant). When pleasant feeling, unpleasant feeling or neutral feeling arises, a meditator must be mindful of it as it is. Some meditators think that unpleasant feeling should not be observed because it is unpleasant. Actually, all kinds of feeling must be noted very attentively as they really occur. If we do not observe or note the pleasant or unpleasant feeling or sensation, we are sure to become attached to it or repulsed by it. When we like a particular feeling or sensation, we become atttached to it. That attachment or *tanhā* arises depending on the feeling or sensation. In this case, the pleasant feeling is the cause and attachment is the effect.

If a meditator practises strenuously and perseveringly, his concentration will become deep and strong. When the meditator's concentration becomes deep and strong, he feels happy and experiences rapture because his mind is, at that moment, quite free from all defilements such as greed, hatred, delusion, conceit and so on. The persevering meditator has attained a very good stage of insight because his mind is now calm, tranquil and serene. If the meditator enjoys it and is satisfied with what he is experiencing, it means he is attached to it, and thus he cannot progress to the higher stages of insight. Such an experience can be attained in the first part of the fourth stage of insight. If he understands that, he should just observe the experience he has attained at this stage. Whatever he is experiencing at this stage, he will not become attached to it if he observes his experience very attentively and energetically. When the meditator notes it attentively and persistently, that happiness, tranquility or serenity will not be manifested in his mind very distinctly.

What he realises at that moment is just feeling that arises and passes away. Then another feeling arises and passes away. He cannot differentiate between pleasant and unpleasant feelings, thereby, he becomes detached from his experience and proceeds to practise for a higher stage of insight. Only then can he go beyond this stage of insight.

If a meditator walks very mindfully, noting the six parts of the step:-

> lifting of the foot,
> raising of the toes,
> pushing the foot forward,
> dropping it down,
> touching, and
> pressing,

and as a result, his concentration is good, deep and strong, he will not be aware of the form of the foot. Nor is he aware of the body or bodily form. What he knows is just movement of the foot. The movement may also feel light; he may feel as if he is walking in the air. He may feel as if he is lifted in the sky. At this stage, he is experiencing excellent meditational experiences. If he does not observe these experiences mindfully, he will like them and may desire more of them. He may become very satisfied with his practice and he may think this is *nibbāna* (the cessation of all kinds of suffering) because this is the best experience he has ever had. All this happens because he does not observe his pleasant experiences, and so is attached to them. This attachment arises depending on the pleasant feeling or pleasant sensation about his good experience.

If a meditator enjoys this pleasant feeling or sensation about his good experience without being mindful of it he is sure to become attached to it. So, he should observe and be aware and mindful of whatever experience he has encountered at this stage. He must not analyse it or think about it, but must be aware of the experience as it really occurs, in order to realise that this experience of the mental process or mental state is subject to impermanence. Whenever he notes, he finds that the experience is not everlasting. When the 'noting mind' becomes constant,

sustained and powerful, it penetrates into
the nature of his experience, i.e. the
mental state. The mind begins to realise
that the experience has disappeared.
Whenever it arises, the mind notes it, and
again it disappears. He then concludes
that this pleasant feeling together with
his experience is impermanent (*unicca*),
because he has comprehended the nature
of impermanence through his personal
experience of the *Dhamma*. Here, *Dhamma*
means mental as well as physical
processes. Because he has realised that
the pleasant feeling or sensation together
with the good experience is impermanent,
he will not be attached to it. Attachment
will not arise when the meditator rightly
understands the true nature of good
mental states or a good experience.

Chain of Cause and Effect

When attachment does not arise,
grasping or *upādāna* will not arise. When
grasping does not arise, there will not be
any wholesome or unwholesome actions,
verbal, physical or mental. The action
that is caused by grasping is known as

kāmma-bhava. This may be wholesome or unwholesome. Wholesome bodily action is *kusala kāya-kamma.* Unwholesome bodily action is *akusala kāya-kamma.* Wholesome verbal action is *kusala vaci-kamma.* Unwholesome verbal action is *akusala vaci-kamma.* Wholesome mental action is *kusala mano-kamma.* Unwholesome mental action is *akusala mano-kamma.* These actions or *kamma* arise through the grasping which is the result of attachment to pleasant or unpleasant feeling or sensation.

When any bodily, verbal or mental action is carried out, it becomes a cause. This cause has its result which may occur in this life, or future lives. So in this way, a being is reborn again through his wholesome or unwholesome action. That action is caused by the grasping which has attachment as its root. Attachment, in turn, is conditioned through feeling or sensation, *vedanā.* In this way, a being has to be reborn in the next existence to experience a variety of suffering because he does not observe his pleasant feelings together with his experience.

Therefore, if a meditatior thinks that feelings should not be observed, he will be carried away along the Chain of Dependent Origination (*paṭiccasamuppāda*) to be reborn in the next existence and suffer from a variety of *dukkha*. That is why the Buddha teaches us to be mindful of any kind of feeling or sensation whether pleasant, unpleasant or neutral.

Mindfulness of Feeling

Mindfulness of sensation or contemplation of sensation is known as *Vedanānupassanā Satipaṭṭhāna*. Usually at the beginning of the practice, the meditator feels the unpleasant physical sensations as well as mental sensations. Here we need to explain again the two kinds of sensation:-

1. *Kāyika-vedanā*
2. *Cetasika-vedanā*

If the feeling or sensation arises depending on physical processes, it is known as *kāyika-vedanā*. We may translate it as physical feeling or sensation, or bodily feeling or sensation. If the feeling or sensation arises depending on mental processes, it is called *cetasika-vedanā*. We may render it as mental feeling or mental sensation. Actually, every feeling, every sensation is a mental process, not a physical process. However, sometimes feeling or sensation arises depending on the physical process of discomfort. When a meditator feels discomfort in his body, then unpleasant sensation arises. That unpleasant sensation is called *kāyika-vedanā*; because it arises depending on physical processes.

In the beginning of the practice, a meditator generally experiences mostly unpleasant mental and physical sensations. But whatever sensation he may experience, he must observe it very attentively, energetically and precisely so that he can realise the true nature of that feeling or sensation. The specific and the general characteristics of the feeling must be thoroughly realised so that he will not be attached to it or repulsed by it. This is *Vedanānupassanā Satipaṭṭhāna* - mindfulness of feelings or sensations. Whenever feeling arises, it must be observed and noted as it really occurs.

It is natural for a meditator to be afraid of unpleasant physical sensation which he experiences in his meditation practice, but painful sensation is not a process that should be feared. Pain is a natural process that should be thoroughly understood by being aware of it as it really occurs. When a meditator can observe pain successfully with persistent effort, then he can realise its true nature - the specific and general nature of pain. Then the penetrating insight into the true nature of that pain or unpleasant sensation will lead the meditator to the higher stages of insight. Eventually, he could attain enlightenment by means of this painful sensation.

Mindfulness of Consciousness

The third Foundation of Mindfulness is *Cittanupassanā Satipaṭṭhāna* which means mindfulness of consciousness and the states (*cetasika*) that arises with consciousness. According to the *Abhidhamma*, every 'mind', so to say, is composed of consciousness and its concomitants. Concomitants here means its associates. Conciousness never arises independently. It arises together with its associates. In short, whatever consciousness or whatever 'mind' or mental state arises, must be mindfully noted or observed as it really occurs. This is *Cittānupassanā Satipaṭṭhāna*. The mental states may be good, the emotional states may be better. Whatever it may be, it must be noted as it really occurs. Therefore, when you have consciousness with lust or attachment, you must be mindful of it as it really is. If you have conciousness with anger, you must note it as consciousness with anger. Consciousness with anger can be noted as 'angry' or 'anger' in accordance with the *Mahā Satipaṭṭhāna Sutta*. When mindfulness is powerful, the anger will disappear. The meditator will then realise that anger is not everlasting - it arises and passes away. By observing anger, a meditator has two kinds of benefit:-

1. The overcoming of anger.
2. Realisation of the true nature of anger (the arising and passing away of anger or the *anicca* nature of anger).

Anger is one of the mental states that can lead the meditator to the cessation of suffering if he notes it with mindfulness.

Mindfulness of Dhamma

The fourth Foundation of Mindfulness is *Dhammānupassanā Satipaṭṭhāna* which means contemplation of *dhamma* or mindfulness of *dhamma*. Here *dhamma* includes many categories of mental or physical processes. The first category is the five *nīvaraṇa* (hindrances):

1. *Kāmacchanda.* Sense desire -desire for visible objects, sounds, odours, tastes and tangible objects.

2. *Vyāpāda*. Anger or ill-will.

3. *Thīna-middha.* Sloth and torpor- sleepiness, mental dullness, heaviness.

4. *Uddhacca-kukkucca.* Remorse, worry or unhappiness about past deeds. Unhappiness at the failure to do what should have been done in the past is the first

aspect. The second aspect is unhappiness about a deed which you did though you should not have done it, i.e., an unwholesome deed which would produce a bad result.

5. *Vicikicchā.* Doubts.

So long as the mind is defiled, a meditator cannot realise any mental process or physical process. Only when the mind is well concentrated on the object of meditation (either mental or physical processes), is it free from all kinds of defilements or hindrances. Thus the mind becomes clear and penetrative; so penetrative that it realises the true nature of mental and physical processes as they really are. So whenever any one of the five hindrances arises in a meditator's mind, he must be aware of it. For example, when a meditator hears a sweet song from outside and does not note it, he may have a desire to listen to the song. He likes to hear this song repeatedly and he indulges in it. That desire to listen to the song is sense desire -

kāmacchanda. So, when he hears any sweet song, he must note 'hearing, hearing'. Still, he may be overwhelmed by the song if his mindfulness is not powerful enough. If he knows that this sense desire for the song can lead him to undesirable events or accidents, or can be an obstacle to his progress in meditation, he will note it as 'desire, desire' until it has been destroyed by strong mindfulness. When the mindfulness becomes constant and strong, that desire will disappear. The desire desappears because it has been observed very attentively and energetically. When a meditator observes or is mindful of his sense desire as it really is, making a mental note, 'desire, desire', he is following strictly what the Buddha taught in the *Mahā Satipaṭṭhāna Sutta*. Being mindful in this manner is *Dhammānupassanā Satipaṭṭhāna* or the contemplation of mind objects, i.e. contemplation of the hindrances (*nīvaraṇas*).

Thina-middha, sloth and torpor, actually means sleepiness. Sloth and torpor is a very 'old friend' of meditators. When a meditator feels sleepy, he enjoys it. If any other pleasant sensation arises in him, he is able to observe it. But when sleepiness arises in him, he is unable to be aware of it because he likes it. That is why sloth and torpor or sleepiness is an 'old friend' of a meditator. It makes him stay longer in the cycle of rebirth. If he is unable to observe sleepiness, he cannot overcome it. Unless he has realised the true nature of sloth and torpor or sleepiness, he will be attached to it and enjoy it.

When we are sleepy, we should make more strenuous effort in our practice; that means we must observe more attentively, energetically and precisely so that we can make our mind more active and alert. When the mind becomes active and alert, it will be free from sleepiness. Then the meditator can overcome sleepiness.

Uddhacca-kukucca is the fourth of the hindrances. *Uddhacca* is restlessness or distraction, *kukucca* is remorse. Here *uddhacca* means distraction of the mind, restlessness of the mind, wandering of the mind. When the mind wanders or thinks about something else instead of noting the object of meditation, it is *uddhacca*. When your mind wanders, you must be aware of it as it really is. At the beginning of the practice a meditator may not be able to observe it. He does not even know that the mind is wandering. He thinks the mind is staying with the object of meditation, i.e. the abdominal movements or respiration. When he is aware that the mind has wandered, he must note 'wandering, wandering' or 'thinking, thinking'. That means *uddhacca- kukkucca* is observed.

The fifth hindrance is *vicikicchā* or doubt. You may have doubt about the **Buddha** the *Dhamma,* the *Sangha,* or about the technique of meditation. Whatever doubt arises, it must be very attentively observed, you must be mindful of it as it really is. This is known as *Dhammānupassanā Satipaṭṭhāna* - mindfulness of *dhamma.* So these are the four Foundations of Mindfulness:-

1. *Kāyānupassanā Satipaṭṭhāna*
   contemplation of the body or physical
   phenomena.
2. *Vedanānupassanā Satipaṭṭhāna* -
   contemplation of feeling or sensation.
3. *Cittānupassanā Satipaṭṭhāna* -
   contemplation of consciousness
   together with its concomitants or
   associates.
4. *Dhammānupassanā Satipaṭṭhāna* -
   contemplation of *dhamma* or mind
   objects.

CHAPTER FIVE

THE SEVEN STAGES OF PURIFICATION

To attain enlightenment we must go through seven stages of purification (*visuddhi*).

Purification of Moral Conduct

The first is *sīla-visuddhi*, Purification of Moral Conduct. Meditators have to observe at least five precepts, if not eight, so that they can attain purification of *sīla*. The third of the five precepts is abstention from sexual misconduct, whereas the third of the eight precepts is abstention from all kinds of sexual contact. If a meditator does not abstain from sexual contact, his mind will be defiled by the hindrance of sense desire (*kāmacchanda-nīvarana*). Only when the mind is purified from all hindrances can meditators realise mental and physical processes in their true nature.

Of course it is better if meditators can observe the eight precepts. If they do not, they may have desires for taste, food, visible things, audible things, odours and tangible things - five kinds of sense desire (*kāmmaccahanda*) in their mind. By observing eight precepts, one can purify one's deeds and speech which is purification of moral conduct (*sīla- visuddhi*). When moral conduct is purified, the mind is also purified to some extent.

When the mind becomes purified, it becomes calm, serene, tranquil and happy and can concentrate on the object of meditation. Then the meditator attains Purification of Mind, i.e.*Citta-visuddhi*, the second stage of purification.

When Venerable Uttiya, one of the disciples of the Buddha was sick in bed, the Buddha visited him and asked about his health. Venerable Uttiya told the Buddha about his sickness:

Venerable sir, my sickness is not decreasing but increasing. I do not know whether I can or cannot live out today or tomorrow. So I want to meditate to destroy all kinds of defilements through to the fourth stage of enlightenment, *Arahantship,* before I die. Please give a short instruction which will enable me to develop my meditation practice to attain *Arahantship*.

Then the Buddha said:

Uttiya, you should cleanse the beginning. If the beginning is purified, then you will be alright, i.e. able to attain *Arahantship*.

The Omniscient Buddha asked the question, "What is the beginning?" He himself replied, "Herein the beginning is purified moral conduct or *sīla* and right view (*Sammā-diṭṭhi*). Right view means the acceptance of and belief in the Law of Cause and Effect (action reaction) or the Law of *Kamma*." The Omniscient Buddha continued:

Uttiya, you should cleanse your moral conduct and right view. Then, based on the purified moral conduct or *sīla*, you should develop the Four Foundations of Mindfulness. Practising thus, you will attain the cessation of suffering.

The Omniscient Buddha lays stress on the purification of *sīla* or moral conduct because it is a basic requirement for progress in concentration as well as insight. When moral conduct is purified, the mind becomes calm, serene and happy. If he cultivates mindfulness, then he can easily concentrate on any object of the mental and physical processes. So purity of moral conduct is a prerequirement for a meditator to make progress.

Purification of Mind

The second purification is Purification of Mind (*Citta-visuddhi*). If we want to attain insight knowledges, the mind must be purified from all kinds of defilements. When the mind is well concentrated on any mental or physical phenomena, it is free from all these hindrances. This is known as purification of mind - *Citta-visuddhi*. With this purification, the mind can penetrate into the mental and physical processes in their true nature. First of all, he distinguishes between mental process and physical process (*nāma* and *rūpa*) through his own experience. That is known as

Nāmarūpaparriccheda-ñāṇa - knowledge of the difference between mentality and physicality.

Purification of View

The third is Purification of View (*Diṭṭhi-visuddhi*). When a meditator penetrates into the true nature of mental and physical processes, he does not take them to be a person or a being, a soul or a self. Then he has purified his view, he has attained *Diṭṭhi-visuddhi*.

Purification by Overcoming Doubt

The fourth is Purification by Overcoming Doubt (*Kaṅkhāvitaraṇa-visuddhi*). 'Kaṅkhā' means doubt, 'visuddhi' means purification by overcoming doubt. When a meditator has attained the second stage of insight knowledge - Knowledge of Cause and Effect (*Paccayapariggaha-ñāṇa*), he no longer has doubts about his past existence. Thus, he overcomes doubt. This is purification by overcoming doubt.

To attain this knowledge he has to observe every intention, wish or want before every action or movement. All actions are preceded by intention, wishing or wanting. That is why we have to be mindful of every intention before every action or movement. When we have an intention to lift our foot, we should note it as 'intending, intending', then 'lifting, lifting'. When we have an intention to bend our arm, we should note 'intending, intending', then 'bending, bending'. While we are eating, we have an intention to open our mouth to take food, then first of all, we should note 'intending, intending', then 'opening, opening'. In the act of opening the mouth, the intention is the cause, and the opening of the mouth is the effect.

Without wishing or wanting to come here, could you come here? Then what is the cause and what the effect? The act of coming is the effect, the intention is the cause. Then why do you sit on the chair? Yes, it is the intention that makes you sit on the chair. Is there any sitter? If you think there is a person who sits on the chair, then we should bring a corpse from the hospital and make it sit on the chair.

It cannot sit because there is no intention. It is only intention, the mental process, that causes an action or movement. So is the sitting posture a man or a woman, a *sāmanera* or a *bhikkhu*? It is none of these. In the sitting posture, there is a physical process supported by the wind element (*vāyo-dhātu* - the internal and external wind element). Sitting is a physical process.

So if we want to sit, first of all, we have to note 'intending, intending', then 'sitting, sitting, sitting'. All the sitting movements must be observed after we have noted intention. When we bend our arm, we must first of all note the intention, then the movements of bending the arm. When we stretch out our arm, first of all, we must note intention, then the movements of stretching as 'stretching, stretching, stretching'. When our concentration is deep enough, by being aware of intention and the actions that follow it, we come to realise that nothing arises without a cause. Everything arises depending on a cause.

Therefore, a so-called person, a man or a woman is just the process of cause and effect. There is no doer, no one that does anything. If we believe that there is a person who does the sitting, it is called *Sakkāya-diṭṭhi* or *Atta-diṭṭhi* (wrong view of a doer). If we thoroughly realise the cause and effect relationship, what we realise is just a natural process. Then there is no 'person' that became a president, there is no 'person' that became a king. Then what existed in the past? In the past, there existed only the process of cause and effect. Then we have no doubt about our past existence. In this way, we can overcome doubts about our past existence - so, this is known as purification by overcoming doubt (*Kaṅkhāvitaraṇa-visuddhi*).

Some meditators find it difficult to observe intention before every action because they are not patient enough. To observe, we must be patient with our actions or movements so that we can observe the intention before every action or movement. When we observe intention before lifting our foot, we will come to realise how the intention is related to the lifting of the foot. Then again, when we observe intention before the pushing of the foot, we will come to realise how intention is related to the pushing movement of the foot. When we observe the intention before the dropping of the foot, we will also come to realise how the intention is related to the dropping movement of the foot and so on. When we come to realise this relationship of cause and effect, we have almost completely realised the Law of Cause and Effect. By this realisation we overcome doubt as to whether there is any personality or entity which is everlasting in us. Then what really exists is just the process of cause and effect.

Purification of Knowledge and Vision of Path and Non-Path

The fifth *visuddhi* is Purification of Knowledge and Vision of Path and Non-Path (*Maggāmagga-ñāṇadassana-visuddhi*). In this stage of insight, you get very good experiences; lightness, happiness, tranquility, serenity etc. Sometimes you may feel your body has become light, as if it has been lifted, or as if you were flying in the sky. Your mindfulness is very keen. Your effort is steady; neither slack nor vigorous, nor rigid. Your effort is moderate, steady and firm. Your concentration is deep, so you experience peace, calmness, serenity, tranquility, happiness, rapture and so on. This is a very good stage that meditators must go through. This stage may be experienced in about two weeks if meditators practise strenuously, but some meditators go through this stage within a week. With such good experiences, meditators may think "This must be nibbana- this is great, I have never experienced it before, it is better than having a million dollars - now I have attained *nibbāna*." Thus, he does not go further because he is clinging to it. He thinks that if he goes further, he will go beyond *nibbāna*. If a meditator holds that this stage is *nibbāna*, this is the wrong path. Therefore, he must continue to meditate and practise strenuously. This is

only a very minor and trivial experience
and he should not be content with it, but
must go ahead with his practice.

Purification of Knowledge and Vision of the Course

The sixth *Visuddhi* is *Paṭipadā-
ñāṇadassana-visuddhi*. 'Paṭipadā' means
the course of practice, 'ñāṇa' means
knowledge, 'dassana' means vision. '*Ñāṇa*'
and '*dassana*' are here referred to in the
same sense. In order to lay emphasis on
penetration, the text used the two words
in the same sense - knowledge and vision.
So *Paṭipadā-ñāṇadassana-visuddhi* means
Purification of Knowledge and Vision of
the Course of Practice. It means that
when we have passed *Maggāmagga-
ñāṇadassana-visuddhi,* we are on the
right path which leads to *Arahantship* or
the cessation of suffering.

If we were on the wrong path, we
would stop at *Maggāmagga-ñāṇadassana-
visuddhi.* Because we are on the right
path, we have to go through the nine
stages of insight and are approaching the
goal, so we can judge that our course of

practice is right. Then we do not have any
doubt about the course of practice. That
doubt has been destroyed by knowledge
and vision of the course of practice. Then
there is purification of knowledge and
vision of the right course of practice -
Paṭipadā-ñāṇadassana-visuddhi. When
you reach that stage, you have attained
Anuloma-ñāṇa (knowledge of adaptation)
because your experience is in conformity
with the lower stages of insight knowledge
and with the higher stages of insight.

Knowledge of Maturity

If we continue with our practice, we
will come to the borderline in a short
time. In two or three thought moments
we have reached the line and stand on
it. The border here means the border
between an ordinary person (*puthujjana*)
and a Noble One (*ariya*). When you are
on the boundary, do you want to go ahead
or go back? If you want to go back, your
attention is towards the past, but if you
want to go ahead your attention is ahead.
Ahead is the cessation of compounded
things, i.e. the cessation of all kinds of

mentality (*nāma*) and physicality (*rūpa*). If you want to proceed, standing on the boundary or border, you look ahead as well as behind. Then you will know, "If I go ahead, all kinds of suffering will cease to exist. So should I go ahead?" You will think about it. The answer is yes, because you have been suffering for many aeons (*kappas*). The word '*kappa*' means countless numbers of existences. When you are at the boundary, you will reflect on your past experiences, "I have been suffering for countless existences in this cycle of *dukkha*. I've had enough of this I must put an end to this suffering."

Your attention is then towards the cessation of suffering. That borderline knowledge is known as *Gotrabhū-ñāṇa*. '*Gotra*' means *Puthujjana* or descendants. On this border, descendants of a *Puthujjana* are cut off totally. Then there is no more *Puthujjana*. Once you pass that borderline, you become a Noble One (*Ariya*) because you have cut off the *Puthujjana* lineage. Venerable Nyanaponika Thera translates it as maturity knowledge or knowledge of maturity because the meditator's knowledge is mature enough to attain the path. Actually, we can translate it literally as the knowledge which has cut off the *Puthujjana* lineage. When the *Puthujjana* lineage has been cut off, the meditator has attained *Sotāpatti-magga-ñāṇa* - he becomes a Noble One, an *Ariya*.

Immediately after the borderline knowledge of maturity, there is Path Knowledge (*Magga-ñāṇa*) which realises the Four Noble Truths thoroughly:-

Dukkha-sacca	The Truth of Suffering
Samudaya-sacca	The Truth of the Cause of Suffering
Nirodha-sacca	The Truth of the Cessation of Suffering
Magga-sacca	The Truth of the Way Leading to the Cessation of Suffering

Purification of Knowledge and Vision

Because he realises these Four Noble Truths, his knowledge and vision of the Truths is purified. So this insight knowledge is known as *Ñāṇadassana-*

visuddhi, Purification of Knowledge and Vision.

The seventh *visuddhi* refers to *Sotāpatti-ñāṇa,* the first knowledge of the Path - *Ñāṇadassana-visuddhi.* '*Ñāṇa*' is knowledge, '*dassana*' is vision, '*visuddhi*' is purification.

When you have attained the seventh *visuddhi* you have become a *Sotāpanna.* '*Sotā*' means stream; '*apanna*' means enterer. '*Sotāpanna*' means stream-enterer. When you have attained *Sotāpatti-ñāṇa,* you have entered into the current of the Noble Eightfold Path. Only then have you attained *Ñāṇadassana-visuddhi* - purification of knowledge and vision.

CHAPTER SIX

NINE WAYS TO SHARPEN THE MENTAL FACULTIES

The Five Mental Faculties of a meditator are *saddhā*, *viriya*, *sati*, *samādhi*, and *paññā*. These five are known as *Pañcindriya* (*pañca* means five, *indriya* means faculties) as well as *Pañcabala* (Five Mental Powers).

Saddhā means faith with right understanding or through right understanding.

Viriya means strenuous effort or energy.

Sati means mindfulness or sustained, constant mindfulness.

Samādhi means deep concentration.

Paññā means wisdom, insight or enlightenment.

For meditation, these Five Mental Faculties must be strong, powerful and balanced as stated in the commentary on the *Visuddhimagga*. *Saddhā* must be firm and unwavering, and *sati* must be powerful and strong, *samādhi* must be deep and *paññā* must be penetrating.

Balancing the Mental Faculties

To make these five faculties strong, powerful and balanced, there are nine guidelines which a meditator must follow. If these faculties are strong but they are not in balance, a meditator cannot attain insight and enlightenment of the cessation of suffering. *Saddhā* (faith) must be in balance with *paññā* (wisdom), and *samādhi* (concentration) must be in balance with *viriya* (effort). The main mental factor — mindfulness, need not be in balance with any faculties; it must be constant, powerful, sustained and uninterruptred.

If *saddhā* is weak and *paññā* is powerful, a meditator may analyse his experience in the course of meditation. While experiencing a mental or physical process, he will analyse it, especially if he has a wide knowledge of the *Dhamma*. When he analyses his experience, that analytical knowledge impedes his concentration. Then his concentration will be broken or weakened. There is no room for logical reasoning or philosophical thinking or analysing which are not right understanding of the natural process of mental and physical phenomena. When a *dhamma* is not rightly penetrated, comprehended or realised, a meditator may have less faith or a disbelief in the doctrine as a result of his analytical knowledge of the *dhamma* or experience. Only after he has completed the practice of meditation and experienced enlightenment, can he analyse it in any way. Then he will have unwavering confidence in the **Buddha Dhamma** and *Sangha* because of his experiential knowledge.

If a meditator believes in the Buddha or the Buddha's doctrine, then his wisdom or insight knowledge is in balance with firm faith (*saddhā*). He can then proceed with his practice without any disturbance by analytical knowledge or reasoning, or philosophical thinking. Some meditators want to display their knowledge of Buddhism or *Dhamma*, so they sometimes analyse what they experience in their meditation and talk about something which is contrary to reality. According to the commentary on the *Visuddhimagga*, faith must be in balance with *paññā* (wisdom, insight knowledge) and vice versa.

When I first started mindfulness meditation, my purpose was to test the technique to see if it was right. Before I began mindfulness meditation, I went through two volumes of *'Vipassanā Meditation'* written by the Venerable Mahāsī Sayādaw. At that time I had not met the Venerable Sayādaw personally.

However, the contemplation of the abdominal movement is very straightforward to those who have learnt the meditation technique from the book. I accepted the technique as true and correct because I knew that the abdominal movement is *vāyo-dhātu*, and the other three elements: fire element (*tejo-dhātu*), water element (*āpo-dhātu*) and earth element (*paṭhavī-dhātu*) are also included in the abdominal movement. As we can contemplate the four elements, this technique must be correct.

Traditionally we tend to favour the method of meditation on respiration or breathing meditation (*ānāpānasati*). I practised *ānāpānasati* in my days as a *sāmanera* when I was 17 to 24 years old. Though I now hold that the Mahāsī Sayādaw's technique is correct, I could not accept it as satisfactory then because I was clinging to the traditional method of mindfulness of respiration. That was why I wanted to test the Mahāsī Sayādaw's technique which begins with the contemplation of the abdominal movement. Although I went to the Mahāsī Meditation Centre and began to practise the technique, I did it with much doubt. That was in 1953 when I spent my *vassa* (rains) there for four months doing an intensive course of meditation. At that time, I was a lecturer at a Buddhist University in Mandalay. I practised under Venerable U Nandavamsa. He told me:-

> U Janaka, you have gone through higher examinations and you are now a lecturer in the University. You must put aside your knowledge of the *Dhamma* from books if you

want to achieve something out of this meditation.

Having accepted his advice, I put aside my knowledge and practised as advised by my teacher. As such, my faith was in balance with my wisdom because I did not analyse the experience or the technique based on my preconceptions or the knowledge that I had learnt from books.

If *paññā* (wisdom) is weak and *saddhā* (faith) is strong, then a meditator may be credulous. We say he is credulous because he has faith without knowledge, wisdom or intelligence, and tends to believe easily any theory or doctrine. If a meditator is credulous, he may fall into a doctrine or theory which leads to the wrong path. Therefore, *saddhā* must be in balance with *paññā*, knowledge or wisdom. In this way, *Saddhindriya* and *Paññindriya* must be in balance.

Then again, *samādhi* (concentration) and *viriya* (energy) must be in balance. If *viriya* is more powerful and stronger than *samādhi*, you cannot concentrate well on the object of meditation. The commentary says:-

> If *viriya* is stronger or more powerful than *samādhi*, a meditator's mind will become distracted and restless (*uddhacca*).

In the beginning of the practice his concentration is usually weak and often wanders. So, he should follow the mind and watch it as it is. If a meditator is enthusiastic for the achievement of insight, he may put too much effort in his practice, thereby causing the mind to become distracted and restless. Effort must be kept in balance with *samādhi*. To do this, he must reduce his effort, keeping his mind stable and steady, noting whatever arises in his mind and body attentively, but not too energetically. Then he will gradually attain some degree of concentration. Because of this concentration, his effort will become steady and firm, neither too strong nor too lax.

In some cases when a meditator has practised meditation for two or three weeks, his concentration becomes very deep and strong, the noting mind notes the object by itself, automatically and effortlessly. If, however, insufficient effort is put in, the noting mind will gradually become dull and heavy. Hence, that concentration changes into sloth and torpor or sleepiness. The commentary says:-

> If concentration is too strong and effort is too weak, then that concentration changes into sloth and torpor or sleepiness (*thina-middha*).

So concentration must be kept in balance with effort (*viriya*). The passive posture of sitting will only make his mind more concentrated on the object and, as less and less effort is required, the mind will become more and more dull. To keep his concentration in balance with effort, he should practise walking meditation longer than sitting. However, only very few meditators experience concentration that exceeds effort. There are also some meditators whose effort exceeds their concentration. Therefore, concentration must be kept in balance with effort, depending on circumstances.

According to the commentary, we can never say that *sati* is too strong or powerful because it is best for you to be mindful of each and every activity of mind and body from moment to moment. Then mindfulness becomes constant, sustained, uninterrupted and continuous, thereby giving rise to deep concentration. When concentration is deep, insight will unfold naturally and you will be able to realise the mind and body processes (*nāma* and *rūpa*). So, we can say that mindfulness is never too strong or powerful.

According to the *Visuddhimagga*, there are nine ways to sharpen these five faculties which a meditator must follow.

The First Way is that the meditator must keep in mind that he will realise the disappearance of mental and physical processes or compounded things when he sees them or when he observes them as they really are. That should be the attitude of a meditator. Sometimes a meditator does not believe that every mental and physical process is impermanent, subject to arising and passing away (*anicca*). Because of this preconception he may not be able to realise the true nature of the mind-body processes. Though he may gain some concentration, it would only enable him to attain peace and happiness to a limited extent. The commentary says:-

> A meditator must keep in mind that he is going to realise the impermanence of existence or mind-body processes if he observes them.

The Second Way is, he must treat the practise of mindfulness with respect, i.e. he must practise mindfulness meditation seriously. If he lacks respect for the technique or the result of meditation, then he will not put enough effort into his practice. Consequently, he cannot concentrate his mind well on the object of meditation. Then he will not be able to realise the true nature of *nāma* and *rūpa*.

The Third Way is, his mindfulness of mental and physical processes must be constant, sustained, uninterrupted and continuous. Only then can he attain the deep concentration upon which he can build up the insight knowledge which penetrates into the true nature of mental and physical processes. This is a very important point which every meditator must follow. While you are awake, you must constantly and continuously be aware of whatever arises in your mind and body as it really is. Be mindful for the whole day without a break. When I say 'sati', it means the constant, sustained and uninterrupted mindfulness and not the ordinary mindfulness.

The Fourth Way is the seven kinds of suitability which a meditator depends upon: a suitable meditation hall, food, weather, etc. Whether or not the conditions are suitable you should make effort in your practice. Sometimes a meditator is very attached to the fan because of the hot weather. He wants to sit under the fan. Actually a meditator must be indifferent to whether it is cold, warm or hot; he must not choose.

Mindfulness is actually the source of every achievement. By means of mindfulness, he can change an 'enemy' into a 'friend'. If he feels hot, he should be mindful of it. If he does so, the heat will gradually become a 'friend'. Likewise with pain. When he observes it, the concentration becomes stronger and the pain may then seem to be more severe. Actually it does not become more severe; it is just that the mind, with deep concentration, become more sensitive. So it knows the pain more and more clearly, making it seem more severe. But when he comes to realise that pain is just a mental process of unpleasant feeling, he will no longer be aware of himself or his bodily form. What he realises at that moment is just the painful sensation and the mind that notes it. He can differentiate between the sensation and the mind that notes it. He does not identify the pain with himself, so the pain does not disturb his concentration. It is like a 'friend'. Therefore, mindfulness is everything, the source of every achievement. Though you know it theoretically, you should also know it practically. By means of mindfulness, you can turn an 'enemy' into a 'friend' A mindful meditator has no enemies at all in the world. All phenomena are 'friends' because they are conducive to the attainment of insight or enlightenment - the cessation of all suffering.

The Fifth Way is that a meditator must remember the way in which he attained deep concentration. He must remember that way and practise it repeatedly using that acquired skill to enable him to attain deep concentration.

The Sixth Way is that a meditator must develop the seven Factors of Enlightenment (*bojjhanga*). You must develop the seven *bojjhangas*, as and when they are needed, they are: mindfulness, investigation of states, energy, happiness, tranquility, concentration and equanimity

The Seventh Way is that you must not be worried about your body or your life. Sometimes a meditator who strives very hard in this meditation from four in the morning till nine or ten at night without rest, fears he may become weak. He worries and thinks that if he continues to exert in that way for a month, he may die of fatigue or some illness. Thus he will not make sufficient effort in his practice and his mindfulness will not be constant, continuous and sustained. When mindfulness is interrupted, it cannot cause deep concentration to arise. When concentration is weak, insight knowledge of the true nature of bodily and mental processes will not unfold. That is why the text says that to sharpen these Five Mental Faculties, you must not be concerned about your body and health. Strive to the utmost, practise strenuously for the whole day without taking a rest or a break, without concern for the body.

The Eighth Way is that whenever mental or physical pain arises, you should strive to note it by putting more effort into your practice. When pain arises, there is a tendency or desire to change position so that it will disapper because you are reluctant to note it. Instead, you must put more effort into your practice to overcome the pain by being aware of it more energetically, attentively and precisely. Then the pain will become your 'friend' because it enables you to attain deep concentration and clear insight.

The Ninth Way is that you must not stop half-way to your goal. It means that you must not stop your practice of mindfulness meditation until you achieve *Arahantship*. Because of your eagerness to achieve *Arahantship,* you will put proper effort in the practice thereby making these Five Mental Faculties strong and powerful.

To summarize, these are the nine ways to sharpen the Five Mental Faculties of a meditator:-

1. Keep in mind the aim to realise the impermanence of the mental-physical process.

2. Practice the *Dhamma* seriously and with respect.

3. Maintain constant, uninterrupted and continuous mindfulness by being aware of all daily activities, moment to moment without a break for the whole day.

4. Seven kinds of suitability must be followed or observed.

5. Remember how to achieve the concentration that was attained previously.

6. Develop the seven Factors of Enlightenment.

7. Do not worry about your bodily health and life during meditation.

8. Overcome physical pain - *dukkha-vedanā* through strenuous effort in your practice.

9. Do not stop half-way to your goal. That means you must always be striving as long as you have not attained *Arahantship*.

CHAPTER SEVEN

THE FIVE FACTORS OF A MEDITATOR

In order that a meditator can make progress in his insight meditation, he must have five factors.

The First Factor is faith. A meditator must have a firm and strong faith in the *Buddha, Dhamma* and *Sangha,* especially in the *Dhamma* which includes the technique of meditation he is practising.

The Second Factor is, he must be healthy both mentally and physically. If he suffers from headaches, feels dizzy or has stomach trouble, gastric or any other illness, it does not mean he is not healthy. He is considered to be healthy to the extent that he can observe any mental or physical process. The food he takes must be digestible (i.e. food which does not cause stomach disorders) because if he suffers from indigestion, he will not be able to practise very well.

The Third Factor is he must be honest and straightforward. That means he must not tell lies to his teacher or to his fellow meditators. Honesty is the best policy.

The Fourth Factor is energy (*viriya*) - not ordinary energy but unwavering, strong and firm energy (*padhāna*). A meditator must have this factor for his success in striving for emancipation. He should never let his *viriya* or effort decrease, but should be perpetually improving or increasing it. When *viriya* or *padhāna* is increasing, then mindfulness will become continuous, constant and uninterrupted. When mindfulness becomes continuous, constant and uninterrupted, concentration will become deep and strong. Insight will become sharp and penetrative, resulting in the clear comprehension of the mental and physical processes in their true nature.

The Fifth Factor is *paññā* or wisdom. Though we use the word *paññā*, it does not refer to ordinary *paññā* or knowledge. It refers to insight knowledge of the arising and passing away of *nāma* and *rūpa* (*udayabbaya-ñāṇa*) which is the fourth stage of insight knowledge. The first stage is *Nāmarūpa-pariccheda-ñāṇa* (knowledge of the difference between mentality and physicality). The second stage is *Paccayapariggaha-ñāṇa* (knowledge of causality or knowledge of the Law of Cause and Effect). The third is knowledge of comprehension - *Sammasana-ñāṇa*. Know ledge of comprehension means knowledge which penetrates and comprehends all the three characteristics of mental and physcial processes, namely, *anicca*, *dukkha* and *anatta*. The fourth stage is *Udayabbaya-ñāṇa*, knowledge of arising and passing away of mental and physical phenomena.

So the Buddha said that *paññā* here refers to that fourth stage of insight knowledge which penetrates into the appearance and disspearance of mentality and physicality. A meditator is expected to possess this factor. In the beginning, a meditator may not possess this insight knowledge of arising and passing away. but he must strive with *padhāna* (strong and firm *viriya* or effort) to meditate on mental and physical proceses to attain the fourth stage of insight knowledge, i.e. *Udayabbaya-ñāṇa*, knowledge of arising and passing away. If a meditator possesses wisdom he is sure to make progress until he attains at least the lowest Path Knowledge - *Sotāpatti-magga-ñāṇa*. That is why the Buddha said that a meditator must possess wisdom which realises the appearance and disappearance of mental and physical phenomena. So these are the five factors which a meditator must have.

When a meditator has atttained *Sotāpatti-magga-ñāṇa*, the first stage of enlightenment, he has uprooted both the concept of a soul or a self, personality or individuality (*sakkāya-diṭṭhi*) and doubt (*vicikicchā*) about the Triple Gem. When a meditator has attained purification of mind, his mind becomes sharp enough to penetrate into the true nature of the mind-body processes. Then he distinguishes between the mental and physical processes and realises the specific characteristics of mental and physical phenomena. This is the first stage of

insight. When he can realise the specific
characteristics of mental and physical
phenomena and can distinguish between
nāma and *rūpa*, he can destroy *sakkāya-
diṭṭhi* and *atta-diṭṭhi* for the time being.
At this stage of insight, he has uprooted
sakkāya-diṭṭhi and *atta-diṭṭhi*. When he is
not experiencing this insight, *sakkāya-
diṭṭhi* and *atta-diṭṭhi* will come back to
him, although not strongly. *Sakkāya-diṭṭhi*
is only uprooted or exterminated by
attaining the first stage of enlightenment,
Sotāpatti-magga-ñāṇa.

Atta in Brahmanism

We should understand the concepts
of *sakkāya-diṭṭhi* and *atta-diṭṭhi* from the
point of view of Hinduism.

According to Hinduism or
Brahmanism, the whole world was created
by *Mahābrahma*. This *Mahābrahma* has
many names such as, *Isvara*, *Paramatma*
and *Prajāpati*. 'Pati' means creator or
master. 'Prajā' means creatures or living
beings. So he is the master of living
beings because he created them.

Paramatma is a Sanskrit or Hindu term. In Pāli it is *Paramatta*. When we divide this *Paramatma* into two words, it is *Parama* and *atma*. Here 'parama' means the noblest, the holiest; 'atma' means soul or self. So 'paramatma' means the holiest soul. Some translate this word as the big self or big soul. This soul is big enough to create the world and living beings. When the condition of the world was good enough for living beings to live in, he created all living beings - men, *devas*, *Brahmas*, and animals. He even created tigers, lions and poisonous snakes, which are a great danger to man. When *Mahābrahma* or *Paramatma* first created living beings, they were like corpses; they could not move, sit or stand. Then *Mahābrahma* wanted to make these creatures come to life. So he put a soul into each creature or living being. Then all the creatures got up and moved, stood, sat and so on. In this way, that small soul or self existed in every living being according to Brāhmanism. Even an insect has a small soul in it. That soul is called *Jīva-atta*. It is everlasting and indestructible and cannot be destroyed by any means, even an atomic bomb, because it is supported by *Mahābrahma* or *Prajāpati*. But when this body is about to disintegrate, that soul knows that the body is about to disintegrate - so it has to be prepared to leave that body and reincarnate into another body. It has to take existence either in a lower or higher world, depending on its *kamma* in this life.If that soul performs meritorious deeds in this life, these meritorious deeds are good *kamma* so they lead the soul to a higher level of existence. When the soul reincarnates into another body, we call it reincarnation. But that everlasting soul, *jīva-atta* or self cannot be destroyed in the next existence either. So the cycle of reincarnation continues. This is what Brahmanism believes about soul. In short, according to Brahmanism, there is an everlasting entity in us, the so-called self, soul or ego.

That belief or concept of an everlasting entity, soul, self or ego, known as *Atta-diṭṭhi*, is due to the non-realisation of the true nature of the natural processes.

Atta in Buddhism

We are not Hindus but we have the concept of a soul, though the concept is not so strong because we follow the doctrine of the Buddha. We understand theoretically that there is no soul or self or that there is no everlasting entity, yet we believe that when a person dies, the soul comes out of the body and stays near his house or his corpse or his coffin. It is a common belief that if we do not make offerings to the monks (*bhikkhus*) and have not shared our meritorious deeds with the departed ones, the soul has to live around us.

Though we believe the doctrine of the Buddha, we still have this concept of *atta-diṭṭhi*, and based on this concept we have another concept of personality, individuality, a being, a man or a woman -*sakkāya-diṭṭhi* (*sakkāya* here means *nāma* and *rūpa*, *diṭṭhi* means wrong or false view). We have this concept because we do not comprehend the specific and common characteristics of the mind-body processes; we take them to be everlasting.

If you ask yourself, "Will I die tomorrow?" - you dare not answer the question. If I say you are going to die tomorrow, you will get angry with me because you have the idea of permanency of mental and physical processes. You think your mind-body processes are permanent; at least until tomorrow. Yes, that is the idea of permanency. You hold it because you have not realised the appearance and disappearance of the process of mental and physical phenomena. If you see the constant, instant appearance and disappearance of mental and physical phenomena, you will not believe them to be permanent.

Theoretically you understand that none of the mental and physical processes last even a second according to the doctrine of the Lord Buddha, but practically you do not believe it because you have not realised their impermanent nature. Only if you have personal experience of the *Dhamma*, do you conclude that it is impermanent. You can then accept, "I may not even live until tomorrow. I may die this very second because every

phenomena is subject to impermanence".
Actually, when a man has not realised the
arising and passing away of mental and
physical phenomena, he takes them to
be permanent. The idea of personality is
based on the belief in a permanent entity
within us. So *atta-diṭṭhi* and *sakkāya-diṭṭhi*
are the same.

If we say, "Now I am lifting my
hand", then you ask me who is lifting the
hand. I will say, "I am lifting the hand."
Who is that 'I'? A *bhikkhu*, a man, or a
being who is living? If we do not believe
in the permanent nature of mind-body
processes, we do not take them to be a
being. But actually, the dual process of
mentality and physicality which constitutes
a so-called person is subject to change,
arising and passing away but we do not
realise it. We take this dual process to be
a person, a being, a dog or an animal.
This view is called *sakkāya-diṭṭhi*. Unless
we can rightly comprehend these mind
and body processes in their true nature
we are unable to overcome or destroy this
false view.

That is why the Buddha teaches us to be mindful of any activity of mind and body, or any mental and physical processes as they really are, so that we can realise the two processes as natural processes. This insight is called knowledge of *Sabhāva-lakkhana* (right understanding of the specific characteristics or individual characteristics of mental and physical phenomena). This insight knowledge destroys the concept of soul or self, person or being which is the main cause of defilements (*kilesas*) such as greed, anger, delusion and conceit and so on. So we can say that this concept of a soul or a self is the seed of all defilements. When we have exterminated the seed there will not arise any defilements and we have got rid of suffering. That is:

Sakkāya-diṭṭhi pahānāya sato bhikkhu paribbaje.

'*Sakkāya-diṭṭhi pahānāya*' means to overcome this false view of a soul, a self or a person; '*sato*' means mindful; *bhikkhu* means monk. A *bhikkhu* who is mindful of phenomena must strive or practise to overcome the false view. When he is able to destroy that *sakkāya-ḍiṭṭhi*, he is sure to deliver himself from all kinds of suffering. This *sakkāya-ḍiṭṭhi* is the cause of all kinds of defilements or the seed of all defilements. So we have to try to exterminate it through right understanding of mental and physical processes by means of mindfulness meditation.

May all of you practise this mindfulness meditation strenuously and attain the cessation of suffering.

Sādhu! Sādhu! Sādhu!

Appendix One

MEDITATION GUIDELINES

Moral conduct

Purification of moral conduct is a prerequisite for a meditator to achieve progress in his practice. Only then will he be free from a guilty conscience and be detached and able to concentrate easily. In a meditation retreat, the meditators are required to observe the eight precepts:-

1. I undertake the precept to abstain from killing.
2. I undertake the precept to abstain from taking things not given.
3. I undertake the precept to abstain from incelibacy.
4. I undertake the precept to abstain from false speech.
5. I undertake the precept to abstain from taking distilled and fermented liquors and intoxicants.
6. I undertake the precept to abstain from taking food at an improper time.
7. I undertake the precept to abstain from dancing, singing, music and

unseemly shows, from the use of garlands, perfumes, and unguents, and from things that tend to beautify and adorn (the person).

8. I undertake the precept to abstain from using high and luxurious seats and beds.

The Meaning of Vipassanā

If a yogī does not understand the purpose of *Vipassanā* meditation, he will not try to discover something by his noting of mental and physical processes.

Vipassanā is a compound of two words: *vi-* and *passanā*. *Vi* means various, i.e. the three characteristics (transiency, unsatisfactoriness, non-self). *Passanā* means right understanding or realization by means of mindfulness of mentality and physicality. *Vipassanā* therefore means the direct realisation of the three characteristics of mentality and physicality.

Note mindfully

Note attentively and precisely.

Superficial noting may make your mind more distracted.

Note the present, live in the present.

If you are looking for something while practising, the mind will be in the future.

The fundamental principle is to observe whatever arises at the very moment it arises.

'Labelling' is a friend of mindfulness when concentration is weak. If you do not label, you will tend to miss the object. Words are not essential but are sometimes helpful, especially in the beginning. Unless it becomes a hindrance, do not drop labelling.

It is important to note precisely every mental and physical process - which need to be realized in their true nature.

Sitting Meditation

When sitting the body of the meditator should be balanced.

Do not sit leaning against a wall or other support. This weakens right effort (*sammā-vāyāma*) and you will feel sleepy.

Sitting on raised and compressed cushions causes the body to bend forward.

This will make you feel sleepy. Sāriputta and Mogallāna did not use any cushion to meditate.

Every sitting must be preceded by an hour of walking meditation (this may be reduced when not in retreat and the time available is limited).

When changing from walking to sitting practice, mindfulness and concentration should not be disrupted.

In the beginning of the practice, a beginner may be confused as to what to note. The Venerable Mahāsī Sayādaw instructed that a yogi may start by observing the rising and falling movement of the abdomen, mentally noting 'rising' when observing the outward movement and 'falling' when observing the inward movement.

This is in accordance with the chapter on the four elements in the *Mahā Satipaṭṭhāna Sutta*. The movement of the abdomen is *vāyo-dhātu* (wind element).

Each element has its individual or specific characteristics.

The Earth element (*paṭhavī-dhātu*) has hardness and softness as its specific characteristics.

The Water element (*āpo-dhātu*) has fluidity and cohesion as its specific characteristics.

The Fire element (*tejo-dhātu*) has heat and cold as its specific characteristics.

The Wind element (*vāyo-dhātu*) has motion, support and vibration as its specific characteristics.

When one is mindful of and realizes the movement of the abdomen, then one can be said to rightly understand the real nature of the wind element and destroy the false view of a self.

In the beginning you may put your hand on the abdomen if you are unable to feel the movement otherwise.

Breathing must be normal. Do not take quick or deep breaths, you will get tired. Relax the mind and body as much as possible.

When the abdominal movements are more gradual and clear, you may increase the frequency of the noting:- "rising ... rising .. rising", "falling ... falling ... falling". If the movements are complicated, just note them generally.

Although the yogi is taught to begin with the watching of the rise and fall of the abdomen, he must not be attached to it. This is not the only object, but only one of the many varieties of objects of *Vipassanā* meditation.

If sounds are heard, note 'hearing'. At first it is not easy, but one has to note as much as possible. Only when mindfulness is sufficient, may one return to the primary object of meditation (e.g. 'rising' and 'falling').

If there is a gap between 'rising' and 'falling', fill it with the noting 'sitting' and/or 'touching'.

Do not open your eyes while doing sitting meditation. If you do, concentration is broken.

Do not be contented with one hour of sitting. Sit as long as you can.

Do not shift your posture.

Walking Meditation

Take the walking meditation seriously. By merely doing walking meditation, one can reach *Arahantship*! Take the Venerable Subhadda the last *Arahant* disciple of the Buddha, as an example.

Bring your attention to the foot during walking meditation. Note the movement with sharp awareness. At the beginning, note the step in one part only, mentally note 'right' and 'left'.

Do not close your eyes but keep them half-closed, looking ahead about four or five feet.

Do not bend the head too low. This will cause tension and dizziness in a short time.

Do not look at your feet. Your mind will get distracted.

When you follow the movement of the foot, you must not lift the feet too high.

The objects to be noted are increased gradually, that is, the number of parts of a step that are observed is gradually increased.

Later one may watch the step in one part for about ten minutes, followed by three parts 'lifting', 'pushing', 'lowering'. Finally it may be further increased to: - 'intending', "lifting', 'pushing', 'lowering', 'touching', 'pressing'.

Please consider this - within one hour of walking meditation, the mind is sure to wander off quite a few times.

You must not look around here and there during walking meditation. You have had and will have many years to look around. If you do so during the retreat, you say goodbye to concentration. Take note of the 'desire' to look around. The wandering eye is a very difficult problem for a yogi.

At least five to six hours each of walking and sitting meditation per day is recommended.

Mindfulness of Daily Activities

Mindfulness meditation is Buddha's way of life.

Awareness of daily activities is the life of a yogi. Once the yogi fails to observe an activity he loses his life. That is, he is not a yogi because he is devoid of *sati*, *samadhi* and *paññā*.

Be mindful of each and every daily activity.

If you canot be mindful of daily activities, do not expect progress.

Not noting daily activities leads to wide gaps of non-mindfulness. Continuity is needed to carry mindfulness forward from one moment to the next.

The faculty of mindfulness (*satindriya*) of a yogi involves constant and uninterrupted mindfulness for the whole day.

Constant and uninterrupted mindfulnes gives rise to deep concentration. Only with deep concentration can one realize the intrinsic nature of mental and physical phenomena, which leads one to the cessation of *dukkha*.

There are many new things to discover everyday if you have constant and un-interrupted mindfulness.

During a retreat, all you have to do is to be mindful. You need not hurry.

The Venerable Mahāsī Sayadaw compared a meditator to a sick person who moves about very slowly.

Doing things extremely slowly makes your mind concentrated. If you intend to achieve something in your meditation, you must get accustomed to slowing down.

When a fan is turning fast, you cannot see it as it really is. If it is turning slowly, then you can do so. So you will have to slow down to be able to see clearly the mental and physical processes as they really are.

When you are surrounded by people who are doing things in a rush, you must be oblivious to the surroundings and energetically note any mental or physical activity.

Talking is a great danger to the progress of insight.

Five minutes' talk can wreck a yogi's concentration for the whole day.

Do not read, recite or recollect. They are hindrances to your meditational progress.

Pain and Patience

Pain is the friend of a meditator, do not evade it, it can lead you to Nibbāna.

Pain does not have to inform you of its coming. It may not disappear. If it does, you may cry over it, for your friend has gone away. Some yogis even induce pain by folding their legs beneath them.

Pain is observed not to make it go away but to realise its true nature.

Pain is the key of the door to *nibbana*.

When concentration is good, pain is not a problem. It is a natural process no different from 'rising' - 'falling'. If you observe it attentively, the mind will be absorbed in it and discover its true nature.

When pain comes it is noted directly but ignored only if it becomes overly persistent. It can be overcome by deep concentration which is brought about by continuous mindfulness.

If there is intense pain while walking, one should stop occasionally and take note of it.

Patience leads to *Nibbana*. Impatience leads to hell.

Be patient with anything and everything that stimulates your mind.

Who said anything is enjoyable?

Noting Mental and Emotional States

If you note any mental or emotional state, it must be done somewhat quickly, energetically and precisely, so that the noting mind is continuous and becomes powerful. Then the thinking will stop by itself.

Note the thoughts quickly as if you are hitting them with a stick:-

> 'thinking, thinking, thinking ...' or
>
> 'sleepy, sleepy, sleepy ... ' or
>
> 'happy, happy, happy ... ' or
>
> 'sad, sad, sad ...'.
>
> not slowly as,
>
> 'thinking ... thinking ...' or
>
> 'sleepy ... sleepy ...'.

Unless you can note the wandering thought you do not have a hope of concentrating the mind. If your mind is still wandering it just means that you still do not note energetically enough. This ability is indispensable.

If you are aware of the content of the thought, it will tend to go on. If you are aware of the thought itself, then thinking will cease.

Do not be attached to thinking and theory.

Insight comes with deep concentration but logical or philosophical thinking comes with shallow concentration.

Eagerness and worry about getting concentration can cause distraction.

Drowsiness can be overcome by putting in more effort. Labelling activities to be noted also helps.

Curiosity and expectation definitely delay your progress. If they arise, do not dwell on them. Give them sharp awareness.

Note sleepiness energetically - by doing it in quick repetition.

If you want to achieve something in your meditation, you will have to put more effort into your practice.

Actually, the energy to note is always there. The trouble is you are reluctant to use it. The mental attitude is very important. Don't be pessimistic. If you are optimistic, you offer yourself opportunity. Then there is satisfaction in every situation and you will also have less distraction.

If a yogi wakes up at 3.00 a.m. he must get up to meditate. He should not wait until 4.00 a.m. That is not the right attitude.

If you are sleepy on waking up, get up and walk. Otherwise you will enjoy sleeping. (In the retreat, yogis were scheduled to wake up at 4.00 a.m.)

If you are sleepy, walk quickly backwards and forwards in the sun.

A human being has a great variety of strengths and the ability to do many things. We must STRIVE, not TRY!

If you put in enough effort, you can achieve the four paths and fruitions.

One week of practice is just a learning process. Real practice begins only after that.

Meditation is beyond time and space. So do not be caught up by them.

The Five Faculties of a Meditator (Pañcindriya)

A meditator must have these five faculties strong, powerful, sharpened and balanced.

They are:-
1. *Saddhindriya* - firm and strong faith based on right understanding.
2. *Viriyindriya* - strong and strenuous effort in the practice.
3. *Satindriya* - sustained and uninterrupted mindfulness.
4. *Samādhindriya* - deep concentration.
5. *Paññindriya* - penetrative wisdom, insight.

These faculties must be balanced to attain insight. Faith or confidence must be balanced with wisdom, energy with concentration. Mindfulness need not be balanced with any other factor. It is the most important faculty that leads the other four to their goal.

Interviews or Reporting Sessions

Daily, the yogi has to report to the meditation instructor to check on his practice. Having given a report of what he did and experienced during the day's meditation, the instructor will correct, give further instruciton or inspire him for further progress. As such, effective communication between them is of extreme importance..

In the retreat, different times were given to each group to report to the Sayadaw.

A yogi should not try to come in before their scheduled time unless he has reason to. On the other hand, it should not be a factor that hinders his meditation, he may come later than scheduled.

When waiting for your turn within the group do not waste time. Sit down and be mindful till called. The next one should get ready beside the one being interviewed.

Yogīs should be considerate, especially when there are many other yogīs waiting and time is precious. Be concise and to the point:

Do not get excited, nervous or afraid. Be composed and open. Speak clearly and audibly in complete sentences. Do not swallow your words, speak in a jumble or mutter.

Do not wait for remarks. Only after you have narrated all your experiences will any remarks be made.

Listen carefully to the instructions and follow them strictly and diligently. If in doubt, ask.

When asked a question, answer it, do not speak about something else.

Report experiences even though they may seem unimportant to you.

Taking short notes immediately after meditation is helpful but one should not make it a point to remember while meditating as this will disturb concentration.

Come and leave the reporting session mindfully.

APPENDIX TWO
RETREAT TIMETABLE

4:00 a.m	wake up
4:30 a.m	walking
5:30 a.m	sitting*
6:30 a.m	walking
7:00 a.m	breakfast
8:00 a.m	walking
9:00 a.m	sitting
10:00 a.m	walking
11:00 a.m	lunch
12:00 p.m	rest
1:00 p.m	sitting*
2:00 p.m	walking
3:00 p.m	sitting
4:00 p.m	walking
5:00 p.m	drinks served
5:30 p.m	walking
6:30 p.m	sitting
7:30 p.m	walking
8:00 p.m	*Dhamma* lecture
9:30 p.m	sitting
10:30 p.m	private meditation

* Compulsory group meditation sessions enforced in the later part of the retreat.

With bad advisors forever left behind,
From paths of evil he departs for eternity,
Soon to see the Buddha of Limitless Light
And perfect Samantabhadra's Supreme Vows.

The supreme and endless blessings of
Samantabhadra's deeds,
I now universally transfer.
May every living being, drowning and adrift,
Soon return to the Land of
Limitless Light!

The Vows of Samantabhadra

I vow that when my life approaches its end,
All obstructions will be swept away;
I will see Amitabha Buddha,
And be born in his Land of
Ultimate Bliss and Peace.

When reborn in the Western Land,
I will perfect and completely fulfill
Without exception these Great Vows,
To delight and benefit all beings.

The Vows of Samantabhadra
Avatamsaka Sutra

DEDICATION OF MERIT

May the merit and virtues
accrued from this work,
Adorn the Buddha's Pure Land,
Repaying the four kinds
of kindness above,
and relieving the sufferings of
those in the Three Paths below.

May those who see and hear of this,
All bring forth the heart of
Understanding,
And live the Teachings for
the rest of this life,
Then be born together in
The Land of Ultimate Bliss.
Homage to Amitabha Buddha!

NAMO AMITABHA

Reprinted and Donated for free distribution by
The Corporate Body of the Buddha Educational Foundation
11 F., 55 Hang Chow South Road Sec 1, Taipei, Taiwan, R.O.C.
Tel: 886-2-23951198 , Fax: 886-2-23913415
Email: overseas@budaedu.org.tw
Printed in Taiwan
1998 July, 35000 copies
EN098-1334